my revision notes

AQA GCSE (9–1)

PSYCHOLOGY

Molly Marshall and Susan Firth

HODDER
EDUCATION
AN HACHETTE UK COMPANY

Acknowledgements

The Publishers would like to thank the following for permission to reproduce copyright material.

Photo credits

p.13 © Ingram Publishing Limited/Scenery Platinum Vol 2 CD 5; **p.20** © Imagestate Media (John Foxx)/Vol 04 Business & Industry 1; **p.25** © Imagestate Media (John Foxx)/Sweets SS107.

Text credit

pp.43–4 Reprinted with permission of The British Psychological Society.

Every effort has been made to trace all copyright holders, but if any have been inadvertently overlooked, the Publishers will be pleased to make the necessary arrangements at the first opportunity.

Although every effort has been made to ensure that website addresses are correct at time of going to press, Hodder Education cannot be held responsible for the content of any website mentioned in this book. It is sometimes possible to find a relocated web page by typing in the address of the home page for a website in the URL window of your browser.

Orders: please contact Hachette UK Distribution, Hely Hutchinson Centre, Milton Road, Didcot, Oxfordshire, OX11 7HH. Telephone: +44 (0)1235 827827. Email education@hachette.co.uk Lines are open from 9 a.m. to 5 p.m., Monday to Friday. You can also order through our website: www.hoddereducation.co.uk

ISBN: 978 1 5104 2594 1

Get the most from this book

Everyone has to decide his or her own revision strategy, but it is essential to review your work, learn it and test your understanding. These Revision Notes will help you to do that in a planned way, topic by topic. Use this book as the cornerstone of your revision and don't hesitate to write in it — personalise your notes and check your progress by ticking off each section as you revise.

Tick to track your progress

Use the revision planner on pages iv–v to plan your revision, topic by topic. Tick each box when you have:

- revised and understood a topic
- tested yourself
- practised the exam questions, checked your answers and gone online to complete the quick quizzes

You can also keep track of your revision by ticking off each topic heading in the book. You may find it helpful to add your own notes as you work through each topic.

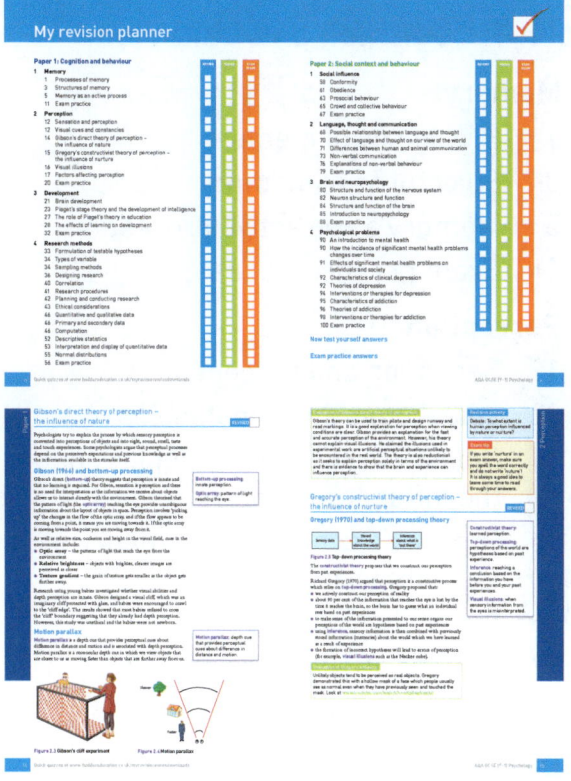

Features to help you succeed

My revision planner

Paper 2: Social context and behaviour

REVISED   TESTED   EXAM READY

Now test yourself answers

Exam practice answers

Countdown to my exams

6–8 weeks to go

- Start by looking at the specification — make sure you know exactly what material you need to revise and the style of the examination. Use the revision planner on pages iv–v to familiarise yourself with the topics.
- Organise your notes, making sure you have covered everything on the specification. The revision planner will help you to group your notes into topics.
- Work out a realistic revision plan that will allow you time for relaxation. Set aside days and times for all the subjects that you need to study, and stick to your timetable.
- Set yourself sensible targets. Break your revision down into focused sessions of around 40 minutes, divided by breaks. These Revision Notes organise the basic facts into short, memorable sections to make revising easier.

REVISED ☐

2–6 weeks to go

- Read through the relevant sections of this book and refer to the exam tips, exam summaries, typical mistakes and key terms. Tick off the topics as you feel confident about them. Highlight those topics you find difficult and look at them again in detail.
- Test your understanding of each topic by working through the 'Now test yourself' questions in the book. Look up the answers at the back of the book.
- Make a note of any problem areas as you revise, and ask your teacher to go over these in class.
- Look at past papers. They are one of the best ways to revise and practise your exam skills. Write or prepare planned answers to the exam practice questions provided in this book. Check your answers at the back of the book and try out the extra quick quizzes at **www.hoddereducation.co.uk/myrevisionnotesdownloads**
- Use the revision activities to try out different revision methods. For example, you can make notes using mind maps, spider diagrams or flash cards.
- Track your progress using the revision planner and give yourself a reward when you have achieved your target.

REVISED ☐

One week to go

- Try to fit in at least one more timed practice of an entire past paper and seek feedback from your teacher, comparing your work closely with the mark scheme.
- Check the revision planner to make sure you haven't missed out any topics. Brush up on any areas of difficulty by talking them over with a friend or getting help from your teacher.
- Attend any revision classes put on by your teacher. Remember, they are an expert at preparing people for examinations.

REVISED ☐

The day before the examination

- Flick through these Revision Notes for useful reminders, for example the exam tips, exam summaries, typical mistakes and key terms.
- Check the time and place of your examination.
- Make sure you have everything you need — extra pens and pencils, tissues, a watch, bottled water, sweets.
- Allow some time to relax and have an early night to ensure you are fresh and alert for the examinations.

REVISED ☐

My exams

GCSE Psychology Paper 1
Date:...
Time:..
Location:...

GCSE Psychology Paper 2
Date:...
Time:..
Location:...

1 Memory

Processes of memory

REVISED

Types of long-term memory

Psychologists theorise that there are three types of long-term memory (LTM) – episodic, semantic and procedural.

Episodic memory is the memory of autobiographical events (times, places, associated emotions and other contextual who, what, when, where, why knowledge) that can be explicitly stated. It is the collection of past personal experiences that occurred at a particular time and place. For example, if you remember a birthday party, or your first driving lesson, this is an episodic memory.

Semantic memory refers to the memory of meaning and understanding and semantic and episodic memory make up the category called **declarative memory (explicit memory)**. With the use of our semantic memory, we can give meaning to otherwise meaningless words and sentences. Semantic memory includes generalised knowledge that does not involve memory of a specific event.

Procedural memory is a part of the long-term memory that is responsible for knowing how to do things (motor skills). Procedural memory stores information on how to perform certain procedures, such as walking, talking, typing, playing the piano, riding a bike. Procedural memories are implicit and do not involve conscious thought.

Revision activity

In pairs, each make six flash cards – two cards for episodic memories, two cards for semantic memories and two cards for procedural memories. Then explain why each card is an example of a different type of memory.

Exam tip

Before answering a multiple-choice question, *read all the options* through carefully before selecting an answer.

Encoding, storage, retrieval

Memory is defined as the **encoding**, **storage** and **retrieval** of stored information. Memories are thought to be encoded in three ways – acoustic, visual and semantic encoding. The three types of retrieval systems used by memory are recall, recognition and relearning.

Encoding (input)

Encoding is the processing of information to form a memory.

Acoustic encoding is holding a memory in the form of sound. An example of this is when we are given a number to remember, we may repeat it to ourselves to maintain the memory acoustically.

Visual encoding is when information is processed visually to create a picture in the mind. If you are asked for directions, you may from memory create a picture of the area in your mind.

Semantic encoding refers to encoding something through its meaning.

Olfactory encoding refers to the recollection of odours (smells), and memory for an odour is long-lasting and resistant to change. Olfactory memory plays an important role in the coordination of the mother–infant bond. Maternal breast odours are individually distinctive and provide a basis for recognition of the mother by her offspring.

Storage

The storage of information focuses on three aspects of memory:
- The amount that is stored (capacity)
- The length of time it is stored (duration)
- The way the information is organised within memory (encoding).

Retrieval (output)

Once information is stored, we may need to retrieve the memory, and this may be done in different ways:
- **Recall** is remembering information as we search our memory. For example, recalling that the capital of France is Paris, or recalling that 8 times 9 equals 72.
- **Recognition** involves us being presented with information and being asked if we remember whether we have seen it before.
- **Relearning** involves us being exposed to something we have learned previously but have since forgotten. Once exposed to it again, we relearn the information, but it doesn't take as long to learn as it did initially. Revision is a form of relearning.

Encoding: changing information into a form to be held in memory.

Storage: holding information in memory so that it can be retrieved later.

Retrieval: locating and bringing back information from memory.

Acoustic encoding: changing information into a 'sound' memory.

Visual encoding: changing information into a visual memory.

Semantic encoding: changing information into a 'meaning' memory so it can be stored.

Olfactory encoding: memory for smell.

Exam tip

A good way to practise your exam skills is to write answers to the exam practice questions provided on the AQA website. Look up www.aqa.org.uk/subjects/psychology/gcse/psychology-8182/assessment-resources

Try some of the questions on a specimen paper and then look up the mark scheme and mark your answers.

Key study: Baddeley (1966)

Aim: To see if there was a difference in the way memory is encoded in short-term memory (STM) and long-term memory (LTM).

Method: Participants learned words having similar or dissimilar sounds (e.g. cat, cab, can, or pit, few, cow) and were asked to recall them immediately (from STM).

Then they learned words with similar or dissimilar meanings (e.g. great, large, big) and after 20 minutes were asked to recall them (from LTM).

Results: Similar sounding words were poorly recalled from STM and words with similar meanings were poorly recalled from LTM.

Conclusion: STM is encoded by sound and LTM by meaning.

Structures of memory

Short-term memory and long-term memory

Psychologists distinguish between **short-term memory (STM)** and **long-term memory (LTM)**. STM cannot hold much information and has limited capacity, whereas LTM can hold an apparently unlimited amount of information and has a vast capacity. George Miller theorised that the capacity of STM is approximately 'seven plus or minus two' chunks of information, but that this capacity can be extended by chunking, or combining, small pieces of information. The table shows some of the ways in which STM and LTM are different.

> **Short-term memory (STM):** acoustic coding, limited duration and capacity.
>
> **Long-term memory (LTM):** semantic coding, unlimited capacity and memory may last a lifetime.

Table 1.1 Comparison of short and long-term memory

Comparison	Short-term memory (STM)	Long-term memory (LTM)
Capacity	Limited (7 ± 2 chunks)	Potentially unlimited
Duration	Short (seconds only)	Possibly lifelong
Encoding	Acoustic (sound)	Semantic (meaning)

Revision activity

To test whether the capacity of STM is approximately 'seven plus or minus two' chunks, write out this list of numbers and letters. Read out each list to a friend and then ask them to repeat back the items in the list in the right order. Could they recall all the items in the six-item list? Could they recall all the items in the ten-item list? From which list were the fewest items correctly recalled?

```
3 6 7 8 M K

4 7 9 5 P R 5

5 7 8 9 L H G 8

6 5 9 G R W M Y F

4 5 7 3 8 Y T S G H
```

Figure 1.1 Short-term memory digit span test

Multi-store model of memory (Atkinson and Shiffrin, 1968)

In the **multi-store model** of memory, Atkinson and Shiffrin suggest that memory comprises three separate stores: the **sensory memory** store, the STM and the LTM. Each store has a specific function, as shown in Figure 1.2.

> **Multi-store model:** three memory stores with different coding, capacity and duration.
>
> **Sensory memory:** very short duration, large capacity.

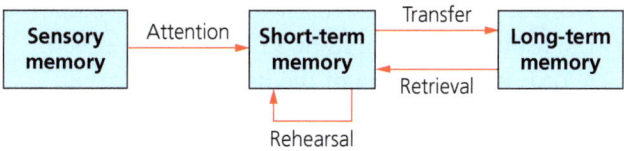

Figure 1.2 The multi-store model

In the multi-store model, information is rehearsed in STM and, if rehearsed enough, is transferred to LTM. There are three stages of information processing in the multi-store model of memory:

Stage 1: Sensory information is perceived (seen, heard etc.).

Revision activity

Write a list of 16 four-letter words. Read the words out to a family member at a rate of one word per second. Then ask them to write down all the words they could remember. Which words did they remember and which did they forget? Was there a primacy/recency effect?

Stage 2: The sensory information is transferred to STM, where it is maintained by **rehearsal** if it is not replaced by new, incoming information.

Stage 3: The information is transferred to LTM.

In the multi-store model:
- **short-term memory** has limited capacity (five to nine items) and limited duration (18 to 30 seconds)
- **long-term memory** has unlimited capacity and unlimited duration
- **decay** occurs because information in memory fades over time until it is forgotten
- **displacement** occurs when information is 'shunted out' by new information and is forgotten
- **serial position effect** – the likelihood of recall of a word depends on its position in a list of words
- **maintenance rehearsal** occurs, which is the process of repeating information again and again in order to move information from STM to LTM.

Evidence for the multi-store model comes from serial position effect studies. Experiments show that when participants are presented with a list of words, they tend to remember the first few and last few words and are more likely to forget those in the middle of the list. This is known as the serial position effect. The tendency to recall earlier words is called the **primacy effect** and the tendency to recall the later words is called the **recency effect**.

> **Rehearsal**: the role of rehearsal is to keep information in STM.
>
> **Primacy effect**: words at the beginning of a list are remembered more.
>
> **Recency effect**: words at the end of a list are remembered more.

> **Revision activity**
>
> Draw a diagram of the flow of information through the multi-store model of memory and include definitions of the key terms.

Key study: Murdock (1962)

Aim: To find evidence for the multi-store model.

Method: Murdock asked participants to learn a list of words that varied in length and free recall them. Each word was presented for one to two seconds.

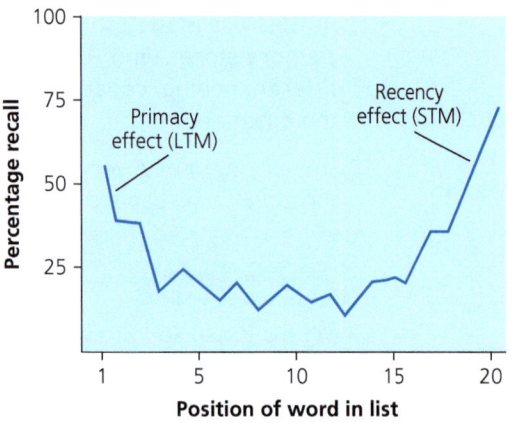

Figure 1.3 Murdock's serial position curve

Results: The probability of recalling any word depended on its position in the list (its serial position). Words presented either early in the list or at the end were more often recalled, but the words in the middle were more often forgotten. This is known as serial position effect.

The improved recall of words at the beginning of the list is called the primacy effect and the improved recall of words at the end of the list is called the recency effect. This recency effect occurred even when the number of words in the list was increased to 40 words.

Conclusion: Murdock suggested that words early in the list were put into LTM (primacy effect) because the person has time to rehearse each word acoustically but that words from the end of the list were still stored in STM (recency effect). Words in the middle of the list were not stored because they had been displaced before they could be stored in LTM. According to Murdock, when participants remember information from a list, the primacy effect occurs when information is recalled from LTM and the recency effect occurs when information is recalled from STM.

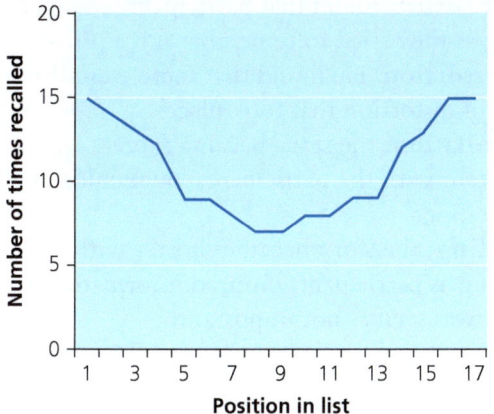

Figure 1.4 Serial position curve

Memory as an active process

REVISED

Theory of reconstructive memory

Bartlett (1932) suggested that recall is subject to personal interpretation dependent on our cultural norms and values and the way we make sense of our world.

Many people believe that memory works something like a video recording with information being retrieved in much the same form as it was encoded. However, memory does not work in this way and people store information in the way that makes the most sense to them. We make sense of information by trying to fit it into schemas which are mental 'units' of knowledge created by past experiences and which may distort unfamiliar information to 'fit in' with existing knowledge or schemas.

According to Bartlett, a memory is not encoded 'exactly' but is constructed and reconstructed to fit in with individual expectations and understanding. In his famous study 'War of the Ghosts', Bartlett (1932) showed that memory is not just a factual recording of what has occurred, but that we make '**effort after meaning**'. By this, Bartlett meant that we try to fit new information into what we already know and understand about the world. As a result, we quite often change our memories so they become more sensible to us and a memory is not just encoded 'exactly' but is constructed and reconstructed to fit in with our individual expectations and understanding.

Effort after meaning: we make an effort to make sense of fragments of memory.

Key study: Bartlett (1932) 'War of the Ghosts'

Aim: To see if cultural background and unfamiliarity with a text would lead to distortion of memory when a story was recalled.

Method: Bartlett asked people to reproduce an unfamiliar story they had read and found that people changed the story to fit into their existing knowledge. His hypothesis was that people store and retrieve information according to expectations formed by cultural schemas. The study used serial reproduction, which is a technique where participants hear a story and are told to reproduce it after a short time and then to do so again repeatedly.

From F.C. Bartlett, *Remembering: A Study in Experimental and Social Psychology.* Cambridge University Press 1932:

Bartlett told British participants a Native American legend called 'The War of the Ghosts'.

One night two young men from Egulac went down to the river to hunt seals and while they were there it became foggy and calm. Then they heard war-cries, and they thought: 'Maybe this is a war-party'. They escaped to the shore and hid behind a log. Now canoes came up, and they heard the noise of paddles, and saw one canoe coming up to them. There were five men in the canoe, and they said:

'What do you think? We wish to take you along. We are going up the river to make war on the people.' One of the young men said, 'I have no arrows.' 'Arrows are in the canoe,' they said.

'I will not go along. I might be killed. My relatives do not know where I have gone. But you,' he said, turning to the other, 'may go with them.' So one of the young men went, but the other returned home.

And the warriors went on up the river to a town on the other side of Kalama. The people came down to the water and they began to fight, and many were killed. But presently the young man heard one of the

warriors say, 'Quick, let us go home: that Indian has been hit.' Now he thought: 'Oh, they are ghosts.' He did not feel sick, but they said he had been shot. So the canoes went back to Egulac and the young man went ashore to his house and made a fire. And he told everybody and said: 'Behold I accompanied the ghosts, and we went to fight. Many of our fellows were killed, and many of those who attacked us were killed. They said I was hit, and I did not feel sick.'

He told it all, and then he became quiet. When the sun rose, he fell down. Something black came out of his mouth. The people jumped up and cried. He was dead.

Results: Bartlett found that participants changed the story as they tried to remember it – a process called **distortion**. He found that there were three patterns of distortion that took place:

- **Assimilation:** the story became more consistent with the participants' own cultural expectations.
- **Levelling:** the story became shorter with each retelling as participants omitted information which was seen as not important.
- **Sharpening:** participants changed the order of the story to make sense of it using terms more familiar to their culture.

Bartlett found that the story had dramatically changed by the time it reached the final student. Participants had altered the story to fit their own cultural experiences. For example, ghosts were omitted and weapons became guns instead of bow and arrows.

Conclusion: Bartlett concluded that memory is constructed and reconstructed to fit in with the individual's own experiences. He believed individuals needed to impose meaning on information they did not understand and to do this they interpreted the story based on their own understanding and experiences.

Quick quizzes at www.hoddereducation.co.uk/myrevisionnotesdownloads

The 'War of the Ghosts' results support the reconstructive explanation of memory which suggests memory is altered to fit in with individuals' experience.

The model explains everyday aspects of our memory and why we do not accurately recall everything. For example, when people remember events incorrectly, this may be due to errors in reconstruction.

The 'War of the Ghosts' findings may lack validity as students may have intentionally changed the story due to demand characteristics or the story may have simply been misheard as it was being told to them.

The reconstructive model of memory does not predict how experiences or emotions will affect memories but simply gives principles of how reconstruction may work.

Factors affecting the accuracy of memory

Interference theory

Memory can be disrupted or interfered with by what we have previously learned or by what we will learn in the future. **Interference theory** states that forgetting occurs because memories interfere with one another. There are two ways in which interference can cause forgetting:

- **Proactive interference** occurs when you cannot learn a new task because what you already know interferes with what you are currently learning – where old memories disrupt new memories.
- **Retroactive interference** occurs when you forget a previously learned task due to the learning of a new task – in other words, later learning interferes with earlier learning or new memories disrupt old memories. Proactive and retroactive interference are thought to be more likely to occur where the memories are similar, for example confusing old and new telephone numbers.

Forgetting due to **retrieval failure** is where the information is in long-term memory but cannot be accessed (remembered) because the retrieval cues are not present. When we store a new memory, we also store information about the situation and these are known as retrieval cues. When we come to the same situation again, these retrieval cues can trigger the memory of the situation. Retrieval cues can be:

- external/context – cues in the environment, such as smell, place
- internal/state – cues inside us, such as physical, emotional, mood.

Interference theory: forgetting occurs because memories interfere with one another.

Proactive interference: old memories disrupt new memories.

Retroactive interference: new memories disrupt old memories.

Retrieval failure: information in LTM cannot be accessed because retrieval cues are not present.

Write your own glossary of key terms for 'memory'. For example:

Bartlett memory assimilation – our reconstructed memories are consistent with our own cultural expectations.

Psychologists suggest that information is more likely to be retrieved from long-term memory if appropriate retrieval cues are present. Tulving (1974) argued that a memory would be more easily retrieved if the cues present when the memory was encoded were also present when the memory is retrieved. Tulving suggested that information about the physical surroundings (external context) and about the physical or psychological state of the person (internal context) is stored at the same time as memory is formed.

Context (external) cues

Retrieval cues may be based on context – the setting or situation in which information is encoded and retrieved. Examples include a particular room or a certain group of people or the way information is presented. Evidence indicates that retrieval is more likely when the context at encoding matches the context at retrieval.

Research has indicated the importance of context-based cues for retrieval.

Key study: Baddeley (1975)

Aim: To indicate the importance of context for retrieval.

Method: Baddeley asked members of a deep-sea diving club to memorise a list of words. One group did this on the beach and the other group under water. When they were asked to remember the words, half of the beach learners remained on the beach, the rest had to recall under water. Half of the underwater group remained there, and the others had to recall on the beach.

Results: Those who had recalled in the same environment (context) in which they had learned recalled 40 per cent more words than those recalling in a different environment.

Conclusion: This research suggests that the retrieval of information is improved if it occurs in the context in which it was learned.

Revision activity

Explain what is meant by a 'retrieval cue' and explain the difference between external (context) retrieval cues and internal (state) retrieval cues.

Exam tip

When you revise, always wear the same item of clothing. When you take the exam, wear that same item of clothing to act as an external retrieval cue.

False memories

If all memory is reconstructed, can reconstruction lead to **false memory**? Elizabeth Loftus argues that false memories can be created during therapy when the therapist tries to help the patient remember things that he or she had forgotten. In some cases, these 'recovered memories' turn out to be false.

False memory: people may remember things that didn't happen because the memory has been implanted, or people remember an event differently from the way it really happened.

Key study: Loftus and Pickrell (1995) 'Lost in the Mall'

Aim: To see if suggestion could create false memories.

Method: There were 24 participants (three males and 21 females) ranging in age from 18 to 53. For each participant, a relative was also contacted. The participants were given four short stories about childhood events that had been obtained from their relatives. Three of the stories were true and one was false. The false story was about getting lost in a shopping mall and being rescued by an elderly woman. The false story included information such as who usually went on shopping trips with the child so that the false story sounded realistic.

Each participant was asked to read each story and then write down what they remembered about each event. A week later each participant was interviewed about the stories and asked to recall as much as they could. Each participant was interviewed a second time and then was told that one of the stories was false and asked to guess which one.

Results: In total there were 72 true episodes to be remembered and participants remembered 68 per cent of these. Six of the participants (25 per cent) recalled the false story fully or partially but 19 out of the 24 participants correctly chose the lost in the mall memory as false.

Conclusion: This research suggests that just imagining an event has the potential for creating a false memory.

Evaluation of Loftus and Pickrell's study

One weakness of the study is that the false memory event (lost in a mall) is not very traumatic and perhaps a false memory for such a harmless event can be easily created. This may not apply to a false memory of an untrue trauma.

Another weakness is that ethical issues arise when participants are left with the implanted false memory. Although at the end of the study the participants were debriefed and told the lost in the mall story was false, even knowing this, participants may be left with a false memory. Is it ethical to manipulate people's memories in this way?

A strength of the study is that it can be applied to improve the way witnesses to crimes are interviewed so that questions are not asked in such a way that will implant a false memory.

Summary

You should now be able to demonstrate and apply knowledge and understanding of psychological ideas, processes, procedures and theories, and analyse and evaluate psychological ideas, information, processes and procedures in relation to:

Processes of memory:
- Episodic memory, semantic memory and procedural memory
- Encoding, storage and retrieval
- How memories are encoded and stored.

Structures of memory:
- The multi-store model of memory and features of each store: coding, capacity, duration
- Primacy and recency effects in recall
- Murdock's serial position curve study.

Memory as an active process:
- The Theory of Reconstructive Memory
- The concept of 'effort after meaning'
- Bartlett's 'War of the Ghosts' study
- Factors affecting the accuracy of memory.

Now test yourself

1 (a) What is the capacity of short-term memory?
    A 7 plus or minus 2 chunks ☐
    B 9 plus or minus 2 chunks ☐
    C 20 chunks ☐
    D Unlimited ☐

  (b) We remember information in short-term memory for
    A an hour ☐
    B about 10 minutes ☐
    C about a week ☐
    D about 30 seconds ☐

  (c) Remembering what you did on your birthday last year is an example of
    A procedural memory ☐
    B semantic memory ☐
    C episodic memory ☐
    D false memory ☐

  (d) Information in short-term memory is encoded
    A semantically ☐
    B acoustically ☐
    C in chunks ☐
    D visually ☐

2 (a) What is the capacity of memory in STM?
  (b) Outline two differences between STM and LTM.
  (c) What is meant by the 'primacy/recency effect'?
  (d) Why does the primacy/recency effect support the multi-store model?
  (e) What is episodic memory?
  (f) What is procedural memory?
  (g) What does semantic memory allow us to do?

3 (a) When talking about memory, what is meant by 'retrieval failure'?
  (b) Adam and Apollo were read a list of 21 words and were then given one minute to write down all the words they could remember. When they were tested, Adam remembered six words and Apollo remembered seven words. Suggest one reason why they remembered so few of the words.
  (c) Explain what is meant by a 'retrieval cue'.
  (d) Explain the difference between external (context) retrieval cues and internal (state) retrieval cues.
  (e) Twenty students were given the names of 20 birds (e.g. sparrow, robin, wren, gull) to memorise and then given one minute to write down all the names they remembered. Ten students stayed in the same classroom for the memory test but ten were taken to a different room. Explain why the students who stayed in the same room remembered more of the bird names.

4 (a) What was the aim of the Loftus and Pickrell 'Lost in the Mall' experiment?
  (b) Who were the participants in the Loftus and Pickrell 'Lost in the Mall' experiment?
  (c) Suggest one criticism of the experimental research by Loftus and Pickrell.
  (d) Identify two factors that may influence eyewitness memory.

Answers on p.101

Exam tip

Allow enough time to check your answers to multiple choice questions. If you want to change an answer, make sure you make the alteration very clear!

Exam tip

When explaining key terms in psychology, it's a good idea to give an example to demonstrate your knowledge and understanding.

Exam practice

1 (a) Identify **one** factor that has been shown to affect the accuracy of memory. [1 mark]
   (b) Use your knowledge of psychology to describe how the factor you have identified affects the accuracy of memory. [3 marks]
2 Briefly discuss **two** criticisms of research into factors that affect the accuracy of memory. [4 marks]
3 You have been asked to conduct an experiment to investigate the capacity of STM. Describe how you would conduct this experiment. [6 marks]
   You need to include:
   - the experimental design you would choose, and why this would be suitable
   - the task participants would be required to do
   - the data that you would collect
   - the results you would expect to find from your experiment.
4 Table 1.2 shows three descriptions of processes linked to memory.

Table 1.2

Holding information in the memory system	
Changing information so that it can be stored in memory	
Recovering information from memory	

From the following list of terms, choose the one that matches each description and write A, B or C in the box next to it. Use each letter only once. [3 marks]
   A Encoding
   B Retrieval
   C Storage
5 Annie asked Sundip why she was sitting talking to herself. Sundip said, 'I am revising and if I keep repeating the same information over and over again, the information goes into my long-term memory.' Outline the model of memory that Sundip is basing her revision plan on. [2 marks]
6 Naomi was in the kitchen and decided to change her shoes, so she went upstairs to get them. When she reached the top of the stairs, she couldn't remember what she wanted to get so she went back to the kitchen to remember. Which aspect of memory as an active process explains why Naomi could only remember what she wanted in the kitchen? [1 mark]
7 **Describe and evaluate** one study which investigated false memory. Include in your answer the aim of the study, the method used, the results obtained and the conclusion drawn. [9 marks]

Answers on p.107

Exam tip

Don't write several answers to a question that asks for just one answer. You won't get extra marks and you waste time.

Typical mistake

Identifying an evaluation point, for example 'the study has low ecological validity', but not following this point up with an explanation.

2 Perception

Sensation and perception

REVISED ☐

Sensation and **perception** play different roles in how we interpret the world. Sensation refers to the process of sensing the environment through touch, taste, sight, sound, and smell. This sensory information is sent to the brain and then perception is the way we interpret the information and make sense of everything around us.

> **Sensation**: the physical process of receiving information from the environment through the senses, such as hearing, taste, smell and vision.

Visual cues and constancies

REVISED ☐

Visual cues and constancies are ways in which we perceive the world staying the same even though the sensory data is constantly changing.

Visual constancy is our ability to perceive that an object remains the same, even when the object projects different images onto the retinas in our eyes. There are different types of visual constancy, for example shape, colour, size, brightness and location.

Depth cues are cues within the environment that help us understand depth. We judge depth in the real world in three dimensions and in pictures when depth is represented in two dimensions. We use depth cues which are pieces of visual information that help us understand depth.

> **Perception**: the cognitive process by which we transform sensory data into meaningful sounds and images.
>
> **Depth cues:** cues within the environment that help us understand depth.

Monocular depth cues are clues to distance that only need one eye. If you close one eye you can still see which things are closer and which are further away. The monocular depth cues you need to understand are:

- **Occlusion**: the position of one object puts it in front of another. It tells us that the thing you can see fully must be nearer than the partly hidden object.
- **Relative size:** a closer object makes a bigger image on the retina than a distant one. Objects making bigger images on the retina are perceived as being closer than objects making smaller images.
- **Linear perspective**: parallel lines in the real world never meet. What seems to happen is that railway lines appear to get narrower in the distance. Lines which are parallel appear to converge in the distance.
- **Height in plane**: a device used by artists. If an image of an object is higher, it is seen as further away than the objects in the lower part of the painting.

Revision activity

Draw a picture and include occlusion, relative size, linear perspective and height in the plane. Label these depth cues.

Occlusion: when the position of one object puts it in front of another.

Relative size: a closer object makes a bigger image on the retina than a distant one.

Linear perspective: parallel lines (such as railway lines) appear to get narrower in the distance.

Height in plane: in a painting if an image of an object is higher it is seen as further away.

Binocular depth cues: provide depth information when viewing a scene with both eyes.

Retinal disparity: each eye views a slightly different angle of an object.

Convergence: a depth cue when the two eyeballs focus on the same object and so they converge.

Colour constancy: the perceived colour of an object remains relatively the same under varying light conditions.

Figure 2.1 An example of linear perspective

Figure 2.2 An example of height in plane

Binocular depth cues provide depth information when viewing a scene with both eyes.

We use information derived from the different projection of objects onto the retina of each eye to judge depth. Each eye views a slightly different angle of an object. If an object is far away, the disparity of that image falling on both retinas will be small. If the object is close, the disparity will be large. It is **retinal disparity** (stereopsis) that tricks people into thinking they perceive depth when viewing 3D movies and stereoscopic photos.

Convergence is a binocular depth cue for depth perception. Because of stereopsis the two eyeballs focus on the same object and they converge. The convergence will stretch the extraocular muscles and sensations from these muscles assist in depth perception. The angle of convergence is smaller when the eye is fixating on far away objects.

Colour constancy is a feature of human visual perception which ensures that the perceived **colour** of an object remains relatively the same under varying light conditions.

Revision activity

Make a wall chart listing the monocular (one eye) depth cues and binocular (two eyes) depth cues.

Revision activity

Demonstrate retinal disparity! Place your pen vertically on the tip of your nose. Shut your left eye and then open it, and quickly shut your right eye and repeat this again and again. See the pen move from side to side, demonstrating the retinal disparity.

Gibson's direct theory of perception – the influence of nature

Psychologists try to explain the process by which sensory perception is converted into perceptions of objects and into sight, sound, smell, taste and touch experiences. Some psychologists argue that perceptual processes depend on the perceiver's expectations and previous knowledge as well as the information available in the stimulus itself.

Gibson (1966) and bottom-up processing

Gibson's direct (**bottom-up**) theory suggests that perception is innate and that no learning is required. For Gibson, sensation is perception and there is no need for interpretation as the information we receive about objects allows us to interact directly with the environment. Gibson theorised that the pattern of light (the **optic array**) reaching the eye provides unambiguous information about the layout of objects in space. Perception involves 'picking up' the changes in the flow of the optic array, and if the flow appears to be coming from a point, it means you are moving towards it. If the optic array is moving towards the point you are moving away from it.

> **Bottom-up processing**: innate perception.
>
> **Optic array**: pattern of light reaching the eye.

As well as relative size, occlusion and height in the visual field, cues in the environment include:

- **Optic array** – the patterns of light that reach the eye from the environment
- **Relative brightness** – objects with brighter, clearer images are perceived as closer
- **Texture gradient** – the grain of texture gets smaller as the object gets further away.

Research using young babies investigated whether visual abilities and depth perception are innate. Gibson designed a visual cliff, which was an imaginary cliff protected with glass, and babies were encouraged to crawl to the 'cliff edge'. The results showed that most babies refused to cross the 'cliff' boundary suggesting that they already had depth perception. However, this study was unethical and the babies were not newborn.

Motion parallax

Motion parallax is a depth cue that provides perceptual cues about difference in distance and motion and is associated with depth perception. Motion parallax is a monocular depth cue in which we view objects that are closer to us as moving faster than objects that are further away from us.

> **Motion parallax**: depth cue that provides perceptual cues about difference in distance and motion.

Figure 2.3 Gibson's cliff experiment

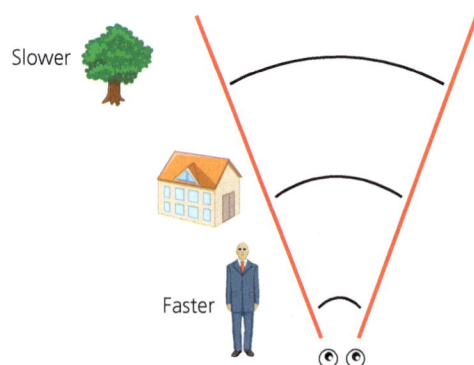

Slower

Faster

Figure 2.4 Motion parallax

Revision activity

Debate: To what extent is human perception influenced by nature or nurture?

Exam tip

If you write 'nurture' in an exam answer, make sure you spell the word correctly and do not write 'nuture'! It is always a good idea to leave some time to read through your answers.

Gregory's constructivist theory of perception – the influence of nurture

REVISED

Gregory (1970) and top-down processing theory

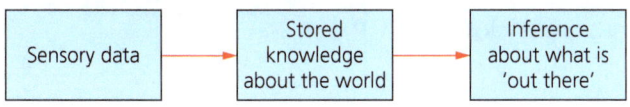

Figure 2.5 Top-down processing theory

The **constructivist theory** proposes that we construct our perception from past experiences.

Richard Gregory (1970) argued that perception is a constructive process which relies on **top-down processing**. Gregory proposed that:
- we actively construct our perception of reality
- about 90 per cent of the information that reaches the eye is lost by the time it reaches the brain, so the brain has to guess what an individual sees based on past experiences
- to make sense of the information presented to our sense organs our perceptions of the world are hypotheses based on past experiences
- using **inference**, sensory information is then combined with previously stored information (memories) about the world which we have learned as a result of experience
- the formation of incorrect hypotheses will lead to errors of perception (for example, **visual illusions** such as the Necker cube).

Constructivist theory: learned perception.

Top-down processing: perceptions of the world are hypotheses based on past experience.

Inference: reaching a conclusion based on the information you have before you and your past experiences.

Visual illusions: when sensory information from the eyes is misinterpreted.

Evaluation of Gregory's theory

Unlikely objects tend to be perceived as real objects. Gregory demonstrated this with a hollow mask of a face which people usually see as normal even when they have previously seen and touched the mask. Look at **www.youtube.com/watch?v=sKa0eaKsdA0**

Visual illusions

A visual illusion is when sensory data is misinterpreted and our perceptual system plays a trick on us. Illusions are proof of top-down constructivist theory and happen because our brain fools us into illusions because of our prior knowledge.

Kanizsa triangle

This illusion involves seeing something that is not there – a fiction. There is no white triangle in the middle of the drawing, but it appears that there is.

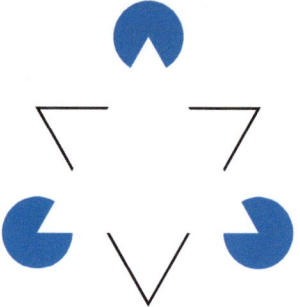

Figure 2.6 The Kanizsa triangle

Necker cube

This illusion is an ambiguous figure. The drawing can be seen in more than one way.

Ponzo illusion

This is a geometric illusion. When you look at the horizontal lines your brain persuades you that the further away line is longer than the closer one, but they are identical.

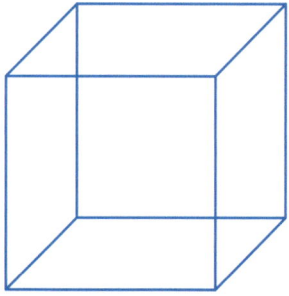

Figure 2.7 The Necker cube

Müller-Lyer illusion

The Müller-Lyer illusion consists of two parallel lines, one ending in inward-pointing arrows and the other in outward-pointing arrows. When observing the two lines, the one with the inward-pointing arrows is perceived to be longer than the other. One explanation is that because we live in a 'carpentered world', the brain is used to interpreting angles as far and near corners and uses this information to make size judgements. Thus, when looking at the Müller-Lyer arrows, the brain interprets them as far and near corners, and overrides the retinal information that says both lines are the same length.

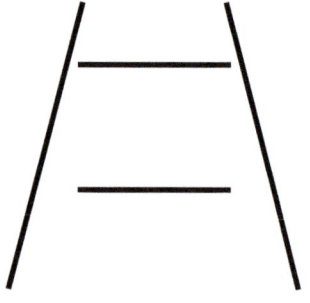

Figure 2.8 The Ponzo illusion

Ames room

An Ames room is a distorted room that is used to create an optical illusion. An Ames room is viewed with one eye through a pinhole and is constructed so that from the front it appears to be an ordinary cube room. However, this is a trick of perspective and the room is trapezoidal. As a result of the optical illusion, a person standing in one corner appears to the observer to be a giant, while a person standing in the other corner appears to be tiny. The illusion is so convincing that a person walking back and forth from the left corner to the right corner appears to grow or shrink. You can view a video showing the effect of the Ames room at https://en.wikipedia.org/wiki/Ames_room

Figure 2.9 The Müller-Lyer illusion

Rubin's vase

The Rubin's vase illusion is an ambiguous figure/ground illusion. It can be perceived either as two black faces looking at each other, in front of a white background, or as a white vase on a black background. In a figure/ground reversal one line can have two shapes. The shape of the contour formed depends on which side of the line is regarded as part of the figure. The observer's perceptual set can also bias the situation making one interpretation stronger than the other.

Figure 2.10 The Rubin's vase illusion

Factors affecting perception

REVISED

Top-down processing is the idea that what we see is based upon our prior knowledge. A number of factors alter the way we will perceive.

Perceptual set

Perceptual set theory suggests that perception is an active process involving selection, inference and interpretation. Perceptual set is a tendency to perceive some aspects of the available sensory data and ignore others. A number of variables influence perceptual set and perception. These include:

- Expectations
- Emotion
- Motivation
- Culture.

Expectation and perceptual set

Key study: Bruner and Minturn (1955)

Aim: To illustrate how expectation could influence set.

Method: Bruner and Minturn showed participants an ambiguous figure '13' set in the context of letters or numbers. (See Figure 2.11.)

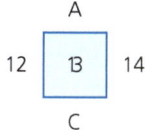

Figure 2.11 The ambiguous figure '13'

Conclusion: The physical stimulus '13' is the same in each case but is perceived differently because of the influence of the context in which

it appears. We expect to see a letter in the context of other letters of the alphabet, whereas we expect to see a number in the context of other numbers.

We may fail to notice printing or writing errors for the same reason; for example, not seeing the repeated 'THE' and 'A' in the triangles in Figure 2.12.

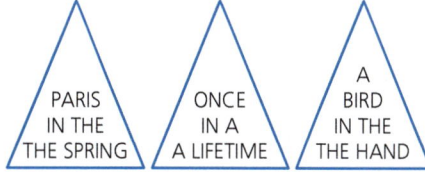

Figure 2.12 Expectation and perceptual set

Motivation and emotion and perceptual set

Allport (1955) suggested the following types of motivational–emotional influence on perception:

- Physiological needs
- Emotional connotation
- Individual values
- The value of objects.

Key study: Gilchrist and Nesburg (1952) – physiological needs

Gilchrist and Nesburg (1952) gave participants pictures and asked them to rate how brightly-coloured they were. Participants who had gone without food for more than four hours reported

that the pictures with food and drink on them were significantly brighter than the others and brighter than they were when they were not hungry.

Key study: Kunst-Wilson and Zajonc (1980) – emotion

In this study, participants were repeatedly presented with geometric figures, but at levels of exposure too brief to permit recognition. On each of a series of test trials, participants were presented with a pair of geometric forms, one of which had previously been presented and one of which was new. For each pair, participants had to answer two questions:

1 Which of the two had previously been presented? (a recognition test)
2 Which of the two was most attractive? (a feeling test)

Participants were unable to tell old forms from new ones, but they consistently favoured old forms over new ones.

Culture and perceptual set

Hudson (1960) noted difficulties among South African Bantu workers in interpreting depth cues in pictures. Depth cues are important because they convey information about the spatial relationships among the objects in pictures.

Hudson showed participants a picture like the one in Figure 2.14.

Figure 2.14 Depth cues in a 2D picture

The correct interpretation is that the hunter is trying to spear the antelope which is nearer to him than the elephant. An incorrect interpretation is that the elephant is nearer and about to be speared. The picture contains the two depth cues – overlapping objects and relative size of objects. Questions were asked such as:
- What do you see?
- Which is nearer, the antelope or the elephant?
- What is the man doing?

The results suggested that both children and adults found it difficult to perceive depth in the pictures. This cross-cultural study shows that culture plays an important part in how we perceive our environment.

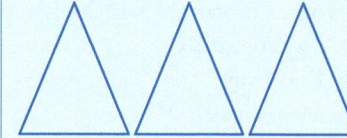
Evaluation of Gregory's constructivist theory

Most people perceive the world in a similar way which suggests that most information is coming from the environment and not constructed by our minds.

Research carried out on newborn babies shows they have perceptual abilities. For example, babies as young as two months appear to recognise faces and complex patterns and six-month-old babies will not crawl over an imaginary cliff despite their limited experience of the environment.

If perception is about experience, then we should not see the same visual illusion the second time because we have learned it is not 'there' and yet this rarely happens.

Summary

You should now be able to demonstrate and apply knowledge and understanding of psychological ideas, processes, procedures and theories, and analyse and evaluate psychological ideas, information, processes and procedures in relation to:

Sensation and perception:
● The difference between sensation and perception.

Visual cues and constancies:
● Monocular and binocular depth cues.

Gibson's direct theory of perception – the influence of nature:
● The role of motion parallax in everyday perception.

Visual illusions:
● Explanations for visual illusions: ambiguity, misinterpreted depth cues, size constancy
● Examples of visual illusions: Kanizsa triangle, Necker cube, Ponzo illusion, Müller-Lyer illusion, Ames room and Rubin's vase.

Gregory's constructivist theory of perception – the influence of nurture:
● Perception uses inferences from visual cues and past experience to construct a model of reality.

Factors affecting perception:
● Perceptual set and the effects of culture, motivation, emotion and expectation
● The Gilchrist and Nesberg study of motivation
● The Bruner and Minturn study of perceptual set.

Now test yourself

TESTED ☐

1 Fill in the blanks.
   (a) Motion parallax is a _____ depth cue in which we view objects that are closer to us as moving faster than objects that are further away from us.
   (b) We judge _____ in the real world in three dimensions.
   (c) Monocular depth cues are clues to _____ that only need one eye.
   (d) Objects making bigger images on the retina are perceived as being _____ than objects making smaller images.
   (e) Linear perspective is a _____ because lines which are parallel appear to converge.
   (f) Binocular depth cues provide depth information when viewing a scene with _____ eyes.
   (g) _____ is the information derived from the different projection of objects onto the retina of each eye to judge depth.
   (h) Sensation is the _____ process of receiving information from the environment through the senses such as hearing, taste, smell and vision.
   (i) Perception is the _____ process by which we transform sensory data into meaningful sounds and images.
2 Distinguish between sensation and perception.
3 Describe one type of visual constancy.
4 What is meant by 'linear perspective'?
5 Sketch the Müller-Lyer illusion.
6 Explain the Müller-Lyer illusion.
7 Outline Gibson's theory of perception.

Answers on pp.101–2

Exam practice

1 Carol touches some fabric and it feels like silk. Which process does this demonstrate? Shade one box only. **[1 mark]**
   - A Expectation ☐
   - B Texture gradient ☐
   - C Perceptual set ☐
   - D Sensation ☐

2 Which is the best explanation for the visual illusion known as the Necker cube? **[1 mark]**
   - A Ambiguity ☐
   - B Convergence ☐
   - C Misinterpreted depth cues ☐
   - D Size constancy ☐

3 Which of these is a monocular depth cue? **[1 mark]**
   - A Motion parallax ☐
   - B Occlusion ☐
   - C Optical flow ☐
   - D Müller-Lyer ☐

4 Briefly outline the monocular depth cue shown in Figure 2.15 and explain how the cue you identified helps us to perceive the distance of objects. **[2 marks]**

Figure 2.15 Monocular depth cue

5 Identify one binocular depth cue and explain how the binocular depth cue you identified helps us to perceive how far away objects are. **[3 marks]**

6 Describe Gregory's constructivist theory of perception. **[4 marks]**

7 Use your knowledge of psychology to evaluate Gregory's constructivist theory of perception. **[5 marks]**

Answers on p.108

3 Development

Brain development

REVISED

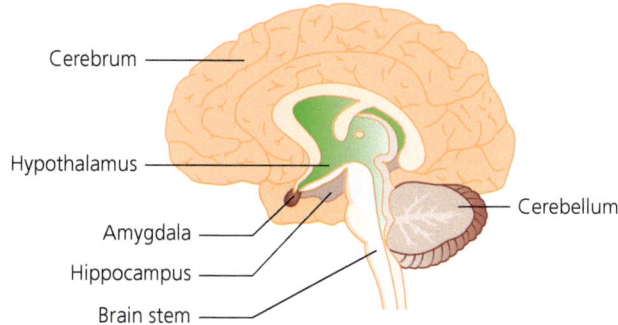

Figure 3.1 The anatomy of the brain

The brain can be divided into:
- the **brain stem** which controls reflexes and involuntary processes like breathing
- the **cerebellum** which is involved in balance and coordination
- the cerebrum which is involved in processes such as memory and learning. The cerebrum's outer surface is called the cerebral **cortex** where advanced activities, such as decision-making, take place. The folds of the cerebral cortex are an important feature of the brain's structure. Appearing during prenatal development, these folds increase the surface area of the cerebral cortex. The ridges are called gyri and the grooves are called sulci.

Neural structures

The brain processes information by forming networks of nerve cells called **neurons**. Neurons communicate with one another using electrical

Brain stem: controls reflexes and involuntary processes like breathing

Cerebellum: the part if the brain involved in balance and coordination.

Cortex: the part of the brain where processes such as decision-making take place.

Neuron: a nerve cell in the brain.

and chemical signals. A neuron consists of a cell body, the branch-like structures of multiple dendrites and an axon which may have numerous axon terminals. The dendrites receive incoming signals from other neurons, and the axon and its terminal branches relay outgoing signals to other neurons.

Brain development in children

At birth, the brain already has about all the neurons it will ever have. The brain doubles in size in the first year, and by age three it has reached 80 per cent of its adult volume. Synapses are formed at a faster rate during the early years than at any other time. At age two or three, the brain has up to twice as many synapses as it will have in adulthood. These surplus connections are gradually eliminated throughout childhood and adolescence, a process sometimes referred to as pruning.

Both nature and nurture influence brain development. The early stages of development are strongly affected by genes that allow the brain to organise itself according to the input it receives from the environment. A child's senses report to the brain (nurture) and this input stimulates neural activity. Speech sounds stimulate activity in language-related brain regions so if the amount of heard speech increases, synapses between neurons in that area will be activated more often. Because repeated use strengthens a synapse and synapses that are rarely used remain weak, a child's experiences (nurture) not only determine what information enters the brain, but also influence how the brain processes information.

> **Revision activity**
>
> Debate: Both nature and nurture influence brain development – be prepared to describe how.

Early brain development

Most of the structural features of the brain develop during the first eight weeks after conception. The first key event of brain development is the formation of the neural tube which eventually becomes the brain and spinal cord. About seven weeks after conception the first neurons and synapses begin to develop in the spinal cord. These early neural connections allow the foetus to make its first movements which provide the developing brain with sensory input. By the end of the second trimester, the cerebral cortex is growing in thickness and complexity and synapse formation in this area is beginning. It is in the early weeks of the third trimester that the cerebral cortex begins to develop.

> **Revision activity**
>
> Draw a timeline showing foetal brain development.

Year 1

Newborn babies can recognise human faces and can discriminate between happy and sad expressions. In the first year, the cerebellum triples in size and this is related to the rapid development of motor skills. As the visual areas of the cortex grow, the infant's binocular vision develops. At about three months, there is significant growth in the hippocampus which relates to memory. In the first year, language circuits in the frontal and temporal lobes become consolidated and are influenced strongly by the language an infant hears. For the first few months, a baby in an English-speaking home can distinguish the sounds of a foreign language but by the end of the first year, the baby's brain has been wired to English.

Year 2

In year 2, the brain's language areas develop more synapses. These changes correspond to the sudden rise in a child's language abilities and a child's vocabulary will quadruple between their first and second birthday. Also, during the second year higher-order cognitive abilities like self-awareness are developing. When an infant sees their reflection in a mirror, they now recognise that it is their own.

Year 3

During year 3, synaptic density in the prefrontal cortex probably reaches up to 200 per cent of adult density and this region also continues to strengthen networks with other areas leading to the improvement and consolidation of complex cognitive abilities.

The influence of nurture

The early years are a window of opportunity for parents, caregivers and communities as positive early experiences have a huge effect on children's chances of achievement and happiness. As experience has a great potential to affect brain development, children are vulnerable to persistent negative influences during this period.

> **Revision activity**
>
> Genes (nature) provide a blueprint for the brain, but a child's environment and experiences (nurture) carry out the construction.
>
> List two 'experiences' and explain how these might have a positive or negative influence on brain development.

Piaget's stage theory and the development of intelligence

REVISED

Piaget believed that the way children learn and develop proceeds as a set of age-related (maturational) stages common to all.

Piagetian terminology

Schemas: according to Piaget, children are born with certain **cognitive schemas** including those for sucking and grasping. In the first year of life other simple schemas develop and schemas are being updated and added to throughout life.

Equilibrium and **disequilibrium**: if a new experience does not match existing schemas, then a state of disequilibrium is produced. The child needs to accommodate to restore the balance. According to Piaget, disequilibrium is essential for learning.

Assimilation: new information or experiences can be fitted into the child's existing schema or current understanding of the world. A child sees a kitten and is able to fit this into the same schema as the schema for cat.

Accommodation: new information or experiences cannot be fitted into the child's current understanding so they either have to alter existing schemas or create a new schema; for example, kitten doesn't fit in with the schema for car, so a new schema needs to be constructed, bringing about a structural change.

Operations: operations are mental transformations or manipulations that occur in the mind. In other words, a child that has operational thought can do things in their head; for example, count. In pre-operational thinking the child needs something 'concrete' to manipulate; for example, they will use their fingers to count.

> **Cognitive schemas:** a pattern of thought or behavior that organizes information.
>
> **Equilibrium:** when all information fits into the child's existing schema
>
> **Disequilibrium:** when new information does not match existing schema.
>
> **Assimilation:** existing schema match incoming information.
>
> **Accommodation:** new schema must be constructed.

> **Revision activity**
>
> Make your own dictionary of Piagetian terminology.

Stages of intellectual development

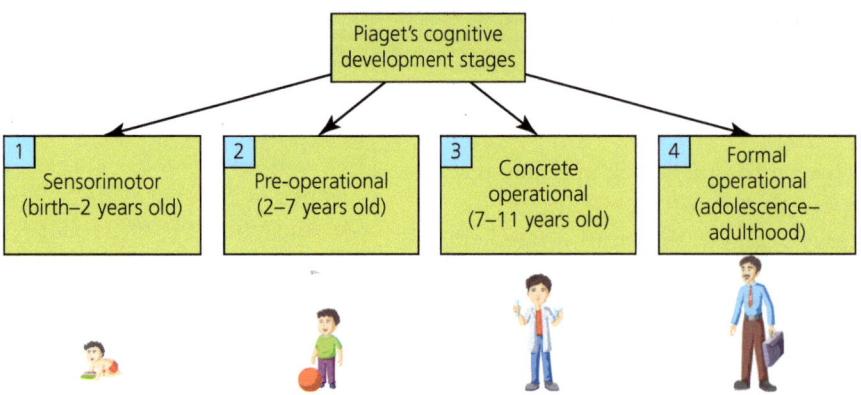

Figure 3.2 Piaget's stages of cognitive development

Stage 1: Sensorimotor stage (0 to 2 years)

A child's understanding of the world is directly through their senses. The child thinks about objects and/or people he or she can sense and/or manipulate, hence the term '**sensorimotor**.' When an object is out of view it is no longer 'thought about' and therefore the child lacks **object permanence**.

Object permanence

When a child has not developed object permanence they assume that an object no longer exists if it cannot be seen. Piaget carried out research on his own children and found that if they were shown an attractive object that was then hidden from view, up to the age of eight months they didn't bother to look for it, but after eight months they continued to search for it.

Stage 2: Pre-operational stage (2 to 7 years)

The child is still dominated by the external world but is now able to create some simple internal representations of the world (schemas) through an increasing ability to use language. The stage is called '**pre-operational**' since the child is unable to perform 'mental' operations. This stage can be subdivided into preconceptual (2 to 4 years) and intuitive (4 to 7 years).

Animism

In the preconceptual stage children may attribute feelings to inanimate objects, so the child may think toys have feelings. Other inabilities include not being able to decentre (decentring refers to the ability to consider multiple aspects of a situation) or to place things in logical order (seriation).

Egocentricity

The child is unable to see things from other people's perspectives. For example, a two year old may believe that if they cannot see you, you won't be able to see them. Piaget demonstrated this with the three mountains task in which children look at a model and are asked to choose a photo that shows the perspective view as seen by someone else – say person X or person Y. According to Piaget, children below the age of seven tend to choose the photo that shows 'their' view of the mountains so they pick a photo of their own perspective.

Sensorimotor: according to Piaget the first age-related stage of cognitive development.

Object permanence: understanding that objects continue to exist even when they are out of sight.

Pre-operational: according to Piaget the second age-related stage of cognitive development.

Animism: a pre-operational child attributes feelings to inanimate objects.

Egocentricity: a pre-operational child is unable to see things from other people's perspectives.

Figure 3.3 The three mountains task

Key study: Hughes (1975)

Hughes (1975) repeated the three mountains task using a situation he thought would be more familiar to the child, that is the naughty boy hiding from the policeman. There were three dolls (two policemen and a boy). The child was asked to position the boy so the policemen could not see him. This was done for four arrangements. Twenty-two out of 30 children were successful on all four tasks and 90 per cent of children aged three to five could complete the task successfully, suggesting that it is lack of understanding rather than egocentrism that caused the problems for Piaget's participants.

Figure 3.4 The naughty boy hiding from the policemen

Conservation

To conserve something is to preserve it or keep it the same, or to *maintain the same quantity*. In terms of thought processes, a child can conserve when they understand that quantity does not change even if it *looks* different. For example, if you pour water from a wide glass into a narrow glass the quantity looks as if it has increased. Young children are influenced by what they see (concrete information) and if the appearance changes they will say that there is more water in the narrow glass. Piaget suggested that children above the age of seven have developed their ability to conserve. The ability to conserve is the realisation that the appearance of an object can change but the underlying quality can remain the same. Piaget believed the inability to conserve was due to two factors:

- **Centration**: the child is only considering the appearance – so, for example, in conservation of volume they focus on the height of the liquid and ignore the width.
- **Reversibility**: the child is unable to perform the mental operation of 'visualising the task being carried out in reverse', for example the liquid being poured back into the original container.

Children have developed the ability to conserve when they understand that quantity does not change when appearance changes.

In classical tests for the ability to conserve, Piaget used quantities such as a row of counters (number **conservation**) and a ball of Plasticine (conservation of mass).

To test for **conservation of number**, Piaget showed the child two equal quantities, for example two rows of counters equally spaced out (Figure 3.6). He asked the child 'Do the rows have the same number of counters?' to which the child answered 'Yes'. Piaget then transformed one display, for example spreading one row of counters out so that it looked longer. Piaget asked the child again 'Do both the rows have the same number of counters?' Some children said 'Yes' (they were the ones who could conserve), some children said 'No' (they couldn't conserve).

Figure 3.5 Why do you pay more for strawberry conserve?

Exam tip

Here is a tip to help you remember what the ability to conserve means – think about why you pay more for strawberry conserve than you do for strawberry jam! In strawberry conserve, only the appearance of the strawberries has changed – the quality and taste of the berries remain the same (have been conserved).

Conservation: the ability to understand that quantity (mass, volume, number) does not change even if appearance changes.

Question 1: Are there the same number of counters in each row?

Then the child watches while the appearance of the buttons is changed (the transformation).

Figure 3.6 Two identical rows of counters

Figure 3.7 One row of counters spread out

Question 2: Are there the same number of counters in each row?

According to Piaget the child who changes his or her answer has not developed the ability to conserve.

Conservation of mass involves two rolls of Plasticine, where before the transformation they look the same, and after the transformation they look different.

Conservation of volume involves liquid being poured from a short fat glass into a tall thin one, where before the transformation the liquid looks the same, and after the transformation (in the tall glass) it looks different.

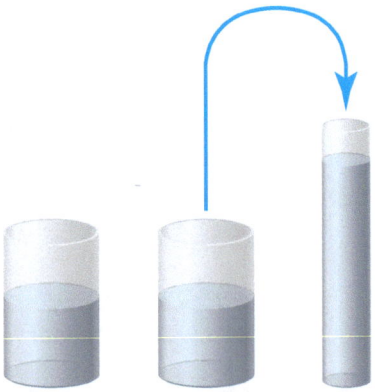

Figure 3.8 Conservation of volume

Key study: McGarrigle and Donaldson (1974)

McGarrigle and Donaldson (1974) repeated Piaget's conservation experiment on six-year-old children. In this experiment the child is shown two rows of equal numbers of counters. The child agrees that the two rows are the same. When a naughty teddy bear messes up the row of counters

62 per cent of children in this age group are able to conserve. This shows that children are better able to conserve than Piaget proposed. In the teddy condition there is a reason for the counters to be messed up (naughty teddy) so the situation has meaning.

Stage 3: Concrete operational stage (7 to approximately 11 years)

In the **concrete operational** stage, the child is now able to conserve and can perform quite complex operations but only if 'real' objects are 'at hand'. The child cannot perform mental operations (transformations). For example, if asked 'If Ben is taller than James and shorter than John, who is the tallest?' without real figures to manipulate, the child cannot answer.

> **Concrete operational:** according to Piaget the third age-related stage of cognitive development.

Stage 4: Formal operational stage (aged 11+)

In the **formal operational** stage, the child can now perform logical operations and abstract reasoning, but according to Piaget only 30 per cent of people ever achieve the stage of formal operations.

Formal operational: according to Piaget the fourth age-related stage of cognitive development.

> **Revision activity**
>
> Make a poster showing the main characteristics of each of Piaget's stages of cognitive development. Collect some counters or Plasticine and with a friend role-play the conservation tasks.

> **Evaluation of Piaget's stage theory**
>
> Piaget's theory has generated lots of research.
>
> Piaget often under-estimated the age at which children could perform activities.
>
> Variations in an experimental procedure can produce very different findings.
>
> Piaget's original studies used questions not well suited to the age range of the children he was studying. Instructions may have been confusing or the tasks themselves too complex. For example, Hughes showed children were able to decentre if shown the three mountains task in a child-friendly format.
>
> In the conservation task, the word 'more' is a possible source of confusion. Adults use the word to mean a greater number whereas children use it to mean larger or taking up more space.

> **Exam tip**
>
> When you evaluate Piaget's theory, remember that in this theory age is the motivating factor in cognitive development. Therefore, this is a maturational theory, suggesting that nature (age) rather than nurture (experience) is what drives change in cognitive development.

The role of Piaget's theory in education

REVISED

The educational implication of Piaget's theory is the adaptation of teaching to the learner's development level, that is the content of instruction needs to be consistent with the developmental stage of the learner. Slavin (2005) suggests the following educational implications from Piaget's theory:

- **Focus on the process of children's thinking, not just its products.** Instead of simply checking for a correct answer, teachers should emphasise the student's understanding and the process they used to get the answer.
- **Recognise the role of children's active involvement in learning.** In a Piagetian classroom, children are encouraged to discover themselves through interaction with the environment instead of being presented with ready-made knowledge.
- **Do not try to teach children to think like adults.** Understand that children's thought processes will be age-related and do not try to speed up development.
- **Accept individual differences in the developmental process.** Piaget's theory suggests that children go through all the same developmental stages *but at different rates*, so teachers should arrange classroom activities for individuals and groups of children rather than for the whole class group.

The teacher's role is to facilitate learning and discovery learning allows children to learn by exploration and experiment. Wood (2008) suggests that the use of 'hands on' experiences help children learn, and practical suggestions include the use of concrete props and visual aids, giving children opportunities to conserve and classify.

> **Revision activity**
>
> You are a primary school teacher and have a class of five to six year olds. Based on Piaget's theories, suggest two ways you will organise your class when you teach a maths lesson. Explain why.

> **Exam tip**
>
> Be prepared to suggest how Piaget's Theory of Cognitive Development could be applied to education and to give one or two examples that could be used in the classroom.

The effects of learning on development

Dweck's Mindset Theory

Carol Dweck's Mindset Theory is a powerful model for enhancing motivation. Dweck suggests that people can have different **mindsets** towards the various aspects of their lives, for example a **fixed mindset** towards their ability to do maths but a **growth mindset** towards their ability to play football.

- **Fixed mindset:** in a fixed mindset, intelligence is fixed and challenges are avoided, because to fail suggests a 'lack of intelligence'. For example, a student may say 'I am no good at maths' and thus thinks making an effort is pointless and getting things wrong and receiving feedback is negative because feedback reveals limitations.
- **Growth mindset:** in a growth mindset, intelligence can be developed and challenges are embraced as the individual believes that they can improve at a task. Making an effort is worthwhile and getting things wrong and receiving feedback is positive because feedback guides further improvement.

Mindset changes the meaning of failure. Failure for individuals who have a growth mindset doesn't define them as learners. Instead failure reveals problems that must be learned from and failure should provide feedback to be followed.

Teachers have mindsets too. A teacher's mindset can influence how he or she perceives the performance of learners. Fixed mindset teachers see those who fail to understand an aspect of the curriculum as not being talented enough to do well in the subject. Growth mindset teachers see struggling students as being in need of guidance and feedback on how to improve.

Mindsets can be changed in either direction and just by knowing about the two mindsets, people can start thinking in new growth-orientated ways. Students benefit from being taught how the brain makes new neural connections in response to learning, helping them understand why effort leads to achievement.

Role of praise and self-efficacy beliefs in learning

Dweck looked at the impact of the type of praise that learners receive. Praise focused on intelligence reinforces fixed mindset ideas that achievement is a consequence of intelligence (nature) and this leads to students avoiding challenges that might reveal that they are not as smart as their teacher believes. Dweck suggests praise must recognise effort. Praise that acknowledges process-related activities such as persistence, practice and study is proven to instil and develop a growth mindset in learners.

Dweck showed how the type of praise given by teachers can affect the mindset of students. Person-oriented praise, for example, 'you are good at this' leads students to attribute their success and, more importantly, failure to something beyond their control, whereas process-oriented praise, for example, 'that was a good way to answer that question' teaches students to believe their success or failure was due to amount of effort.

Self-efficacy refers to a student's belief about their ability to successfully complete a task. For example, a student may feel confident that they can learn psychology but believe they will never be good at maths.

> **Mindset:** Carol Dweck's theory in which mindset is an attitude towards an aspect of life.
>
> **Fixed mindset:** the belief that some aspect of intelligence is fixed.
>
> **Growth mindset:** the belief that some aspect of intelligence can be developed.

> **Revision activity**
>
> Think about your own mindset and remind yourself that effective revision will pay dividends in the exam.

> **Self-efficacy:** belief about one's ability to successfully complete a task.

Key study: Hattie and Marzano (2001)

Hattie and Marzano (2001) found that students' self-efficacy had a substantial impact on their subsequent achievement. Students who believed they would master fractions were more likely to do so, while students who believed they were poor readers were less likely to improve their reading. Research showed that teachers can build students' self-efficacy through praise and expressing belief that they can do well. However, to be effective, such praise must:

- be genuine and only given when students have made real improvement
- refer to specific accomplishments related to the task.

Hattie highlighted the fact that the link between self-efficacy and achievement is reciprocal. That is, achieving genuine success has as much impact on subsequent self-efficacy, as self-efficacy has on subsequent achievement.

Learning styles including verbalisers and visualisers

The preferred way in which an individual approaches a learning situation (their learning style) has been characterised in several different ways. The verbaliser–visualiser dimension describes the degree to which individuals tend to represent information as words (**verbaliser**) or as images (**visualiser**).

> **Verbaliser:** an individual who represents information as words.
>
> **Visualiser:** an individual who represents information as images.

Paivio's verbaliser–visualiser cognitive style

The assertion that individuals process information either verbally or visually originates from the dual coding theory (Paivio, 1971). The verbaliser–visualiser learning style is assessed through tests that examine an individual's ability to generate information not present but dependent upon the presence of an image. Individuals who respond quickly are considered visualisers and those with slower response rates as verbalisers. Some research suggests that verbalisers learn best from text-based material and visualisers from pictorially presented material. This suggests that if there is a mismatch between a student's preferred learning style and the way information to be learned is presented, learning will be adversely affected.

> **Revision activity**
>
> Design a task to find out whether people are verbalisers or visualisers.

Willingham's Learning Theory

Daniel Willingham has criticised the theory of learning styles as unsupported by evidence. He advocates teaching students scientifically-proven study habits.

According to Willingham: 'Some lessons click with one child and not with another – not because of a predisposition in the way the child learns but because of the knowledge the child brought to the lesson, his interests, or other factors.'

Willingham (2012) suggests that teachers should use the content's best modality (**content modality**), not search for the students' best modality (**learner modality**). If the teacher wants students to learn what something looks like, then the presentation should be visual. For example, if students are to learn about Egyptian pyramids, seeing a picture is more effective than hearing a verbal description. If students are to learn the form of an English sonnet, they should hear the stress forms of iambic pentameter, and then see a visual representation of it.

> **Content modality:** the characteristics of what is to be learned.
>
> **Learner modality:** the individual's learning style.

Willingham asserts that material should be presented verbally or visually because the information that the teacher wants students to understand is best conveyed in that modality. There is no benefit to students in teachers attempting to find verbal presentations of pictorial information, and modality matters in the same way for all students.

(Taken from https://larrycuban.wordpress.com/2012/04/15/student-learning-styles-theory-is-bunk-daniel-willingham/)

Summary

You should now be able to demonstrate and apply knowledge and understanding of psychological ideas, processes, procedures and theories, and analyse and evaluate psychological ideas, information, processes and procedures in relation to:

Early brain development:
- Neural structures in brain stem, thalamus, cerebellum and cortex
- The development of autonomic functions, sensory processing, movement and cognition
- The roles of nature and nurture.

Piaget's stage theory and the development of intelligence:
- The concepts of assimilation and accommodation.

The role of Piaget's theory in education:
- The stages of sensorimotor, pre-operational, concrete operational and formal operational development and the application of these stages in education
- Reduction of egocentricity, the development of conservation
- McGarrigle and Donaldson's 'naughty teddy study'
- Hughes' 'policeman doll study'.

The effects of learning on development:
- Dweck's Mindset Theory of learning; fixed mindset and growth mindset
- The role of praise and self-efficacy beliefs in learning
- Learning styles including verbalisers and visualisers
- Willingham's Learning Theory and his criticism of learning styles.

Now test yourself

TESTED ☐

1 Which part of the brain is involved in decision-making?
- A The brain stem ☐
- B The cerebral cortex ☐
- C The neural tube ☐
- D The dendrites ☐

2 Which of the options below are correct?
- A Dendrites receive incoming signals and axons relay outgoing signals to other neurons. ☐
- B Dendrites send outgoing signals and axons relay incoming signals to other neurons. ☐
- C Both axons and dendrites receive incoming signals. ☐
- D Both axons and dendrites send outgoing signals. ☐

3 Which of the following is **true**?
- A At the age of three, the brain has up to twice as many synapses as it has at the age of 20. ☐
- B At the age of three, the brain has half as many synapses as it has at the age of 20. ☐
- C At the age of three, the brain has 70 per cent fewer synapses than it has at the age of 20. ☐
- D At the age of three, the brain has 10 per cent more synapses than it has at the age of 20. ☐

4 How many stages of cognitive development did Piaget propose?
- A Five ☐
- B Four ☐
- C Three ☐
- D Six ☐

5 A child who is not able to see things from the perspective of another person is:
- A Egocentric ☐
- B Selfish ☐
- C Unable to decentre ☐
- D Gender biased ☐

→

6 Fill in the blanks.
   (a) A schema is a _____ structure and as we age we develop schemas for abstract concepts.
   (b) Piaget proposed that if new experience does not match existing schemas a state of _____ is produced.
   (c) _____ occurs when new information can be fitted into the child's current understanding of the world.
   (d) The ability to _____ has been developed when a child understands that quantity does not change when appearance changes.

7 In Piaget's theory, which one of the following sequences shows the order of the stages of cognitive development?
   A Sensorimotor, concrete operational, pre-operational, formal operational ☐
   B Sensorimotor, pre-operational, concrete operational, formal operational ☐
   C Pre-operational, sensorimotor, concrete operational, formal operational ☐
   D Concrete operational, sensorimotor, pre-operational, formal operational ☐

8 Which one of the following statements describes a child who has not developed object permanence?
   A The inability to understand abstract and hypothetical ideas ☐
   B The inability to understand that people still exist when out of sight ☐
   C The inability to understand things are the same even if they look different ☐
   D The inability to understand things from different points of view ☐

9 Which one of the following statements describes a feature of Piaget's concrete operational stage?
   A Unable to see the world from another person's point of view ☐
   B Unable to understand that people still exist when out of sight ☐
   C Does not understand that the quality of an object remains the same if its appearance changes ☐
   D Unable to perform mental transformations without a real object to manipulate ☐

10 In the McGarrigle and Donaldson (1974) study, what did 'naughty teddy' do?
   A Steal the chocolate counters ☐
   B Eat the biscuit ☐
   C Mess up the rows of counters ☐
   D Spill the juice ☐

11 Which of these is Dweck's Mindset Theory of learning?
   A Fixed and growth mindset ☐
   B Fixed and learning mindset ☐
   C Growth and stable mindset ☐
   D Fixed and developing mindset ☐

12 Willingham (2012) suggests that to maximise learning teachers should use:
   A the students' preferred learning style ☐
   B pictures rather than words ☐
   C text-based information ☐
   D the content's best modality ☐

Answers on p.102

Exam practice

1 Which of the following describes one feature that is **not** usually present by the end of Piaget's pre-operational stage of development? Shade one box only. **[1 mark]**

   A The child thinks in an abstract way. ☐

   B The child understands objects exist when they are out of sight. ☐

   C The child understands the difference between animate and inanimate objects. ☐

   D The child understands things from a different point of view. ☐

2 Which of these age ranges would best fit a child who can't understand that there is the same amount of orange juice in a short wide glass as there is in a tall thin glass? **[1 mark]**

   A 1–2 ☐

   B 2–7 ☐

   C 5–11 ☐

   D 3–4 ☐

3 Suggest **one** way in which Piaget's Theory of Cognitive Development could be applied to education, and support your answer with an example that could be used in the classroom. **[2 marks]**

4 Identify and explain **one** criticism of Piaget's Theory of Cognitive Development. **[4 marks]**

5 (a) Michelle wasn't going to bother to revise for her GCSE maths exam because as she explained, 'I am not very clever at maths and never will be.' Identify Michelle's likely mindset. **[1 mark]**

   (b) How can Dweck's Mindset Theory explain Michelle's decision not to revise for her GCSE maths exam? **[6 marks]**

6 Two students are discussing their progress in French at GCSE. Read their conversation below and then answer the question that follows.

   Phyliss said, 'You'll get an A because you were born good at learning languages, but I wasn't so there's no point me trying.' Benito said, 'You're wrong! I wasn't any good at first, but I've practised and practised my French and that's why I'm better now, but it's been hard work.'

   Outline and evaluate Dweck's Mindset Theory of learning. Refer to the conversation between Phyliss and Benito in your answer. **[9 marks]**

7 (a) Explain what is meant by having a 'learning style'. **[1 mark]**

   (b) Outline and evaluate the theory that students are either verbalisers or visualisers. **[6 marks]**

Answers on p.108

> **Exam tip**
>
> Watch out for questions like question 4. This question asks you to identify the criticism and explain it so make sure you do both!

4 Research methods

Formulation of testable hypotheses

REVISED

A **hypothesis** states precisely what the researcher believes to be true about the target population. It is often generated from a theory and is a testable statement.
- The **alternative hypothesis** states that some difference (or effect) will occur; that the independent variable (IV) will have a significant effect on the dependent variable (DV).
- The **null hypothesis** is a statement of no difference (or of no correlation); in effect, it says the IV does not affect the DV. If data analysis forces researchers to reject the null hypothesis, because a significant effect is found, they then accept the alternative hypothesis.

Revision activity

Practise writing alternative and null hypotheses.

Typical mistake

Confusing the alternative hypothesis with the null hypothesis.

Types of variable

The **independent variable** (IV) is the variable we manipulate in experimental research. The **dependent variable** (DV) is the variable we measure in experimental research.

Operationalisation of variables means being able to define variables in order to manipulate the IV and measure the DV; for example, performance in a memory test might be operationalised as 'the number of words remembered'.

Extraneous variables are any variables that have not been controlled and that may have an effect on the IV or the DV. Extraneous variables are variables, other than the IV, that change between the conditions and are difficult to control (for example, how hungry the participants are). Controls should be used to try to avoid variables other than the IV from affecting the DV. Controls can include random allocation of participants to experimental conditions to distribute individual differences within the sample equally between conditions.

> **Typical mistake**
>
> Confusing the IV with the DV. Make sure you can define both and know which is which.

Sampling methods

When researchers conduct research, the **target population** is the group of people to whom they wish to generalise their findings. The **sample** of participants is the group of people who take part in the study, and a **representative sample** is a sample of people who are representative of the target population. There are several ways in which researchers select a sample.

Random sampling

This involves having the names of the target population and giving everyone an equal chance of being selected. A random sample can be selected by a computer or, in a small population, by selecting names from a hat.

> **Strength:** a true random sample avoids bias, as every member of the target population has an equal chance of being selected.
>
> **Weakness:** it is almost impossible to obtain a truly random sample because not all the names of the target population may be known.

Opportunity sampling

This involves asking whoever is available and willing to participate. An opportunity sample is not likely to be representative of any target population because it will probably comprise friends of the researcher, or students, or people in a specific workplace. The people approached will be those who are local and available.

> **Typical mistake**
>
> Telling the examiner that an opportunity sample of people who are approached in a street is a random sample.

> **Strength:** researchers can quickly and inexpensively acquire a sample, and face-to-face ethical briefings and debriefings can be undertaken.
>
> **Weakness:** opportunity samples are almost always biased samples, as who participates is dependent on who is asked and who happens to be available locally at the time.

Systematic sampling

A systematic sample selects participants in a systematic way from the target population, for example every tenth participant on a list of names. To take a systematic sample, you list all the members of the population and then decide on a sample size. By dividing the number of people in the population by the number of people you want in your sample, you get a number and then you take every nth participant to get a systematic sample.

> **Strength:** systematic sampling should provide a representative sample.
>
> **Weakness:** this method is only possible if you can identify all members of the population to be studied.

Stratified sampling

In stratified sampling the researcher identifies the different types of people that make up the target population and works out the proportions needed for the sample to be representative.

A list is made of each variable of interest (for example, gender, age group, occupation), which might have an effect on the research. For example, if we are interested in why some people donate to a charity and some don't, gender, age, and income may be important, so we work out the relative percentage of each group in our population of interest. The sample must then contain all these groups in the same proportion as in the target population.

> **Strength:** a stratified sample should be highly representative of the target population and therefore we can generalise from the results obtained.
>
> **Weakness:** gathering such a sample is time-consuming and difficult to carry out and therefore this method is rarely used.

Revision activity

Make a set of sampling flash cards with the sampling technique named on one side and instructions on how to gain this type of sample on the other side.

Principles of sampling applied to scientific data

The sample of participants should be a true representation of diversity in the target population. A scientific sample should not be biased. For example, an all-student sample is a biased sample, only representative of a target population of students. Likewise, an all-male sample is a biased sample and only representative of an all-male target population.

One of the principles of science is generalisation. When scientists generalise, they draw inferences from particular observations and if the sample is not representative, the research findings cannot be generalised to the target population. The size of the sample is also important, and the sample must be large enough to be representative of the target population. However, a very large sample makes research time-consuming and in small samples any differences between participants will have a greater effect.

Designing research

Quantitative and qualitative methods

Quantitative research uses methods that measure amounts of behaviour, usually by assigning a numeric value to what is being measured (the quantity).

Qualitative research measures what behaviour is like (the quality) and usually results in descriptive data.

Experimental method

Laboratory experiments: a laboratory experiment is a method of conducting research in which researchers try to control all the variables except the one that is changed between the experimental conditions. The variable that is changed is called the independent variable (IV) and the effect it may have is called the dependent variable (DV).

Table 4.1 Strengths and weaknesses of laboratory experiments

Strength	Weakness
High levels of control in a laboratory experiment allow extraneous variables that might affect the IV or the DV to be minimised. The researcher can be sure that any changes in the DV are the result of changes in the IV.	Laboratory experiments may not measure how people behave outside in their everyday lives.
High levels of control make it possible to measure the effect of one variable on another. Statements about cause and effect can be made.	Aspects of the experiment may cause the participants (and the experimenter) to change the way they behave (demand characteristics). This can mean that it is not the effect of the IV that is measured, leading to invalid results.
Laboratory experiments can be replicated to check the findings.	

Field experiments: a field experiment is a way of conducting research in an everyday environment (for example, in a school or hospital), where one or more IVs are manipulated by the experimenter and the effect on the DV is measured. One difference between laboratory and field experiments is an increase in the naturalness of the setting and a decrease in the level of control that the experimenter can achieve.

Table 4.2 Strengths and weaknesses of field experiments

Strength	Weakness
Field experiments allow psychologists to measure how people behave in their everyday lives.	It is not always possible to control for extraneous variables that might affect the IV or the DV, so the researcher cannot always be sure that any changes in the DV are the result of changes in the IV.
Manipulation of the IV and some level of control make it possible to measure the effect of one variable on another.	Field experiments can be difficult to replicate; therefore, it may not be possible to check the reliability of the findings.
If participants do not know they are participating in a study, they will be unaware that they are being watched and this reduces the probability that their behaviour results from demand characteristics.	Participants may not be asked for informed consent which breaches the British Psychological Society's ethical guidelines.

Natural experiments: a natural experiment is one in which, rather than being manipulated by the researcher, the IV to be studied is naturally occurring. Some examples of naturally occurring variables are gender, age, ethnicity and occupation. When the IV is naturally occurring, participants cannot be randomly allocated between conditions.

Table 4.3 Strengths and weaknesses of natural experiments

Strength	Weakness
Natural experiments allow psychologists to study the effects of IVs that could be unethical to manipulate.	Since participants cannot be allocated randomly between conditions, individual differences other than the IV can also affect the DV. This may lead to low internal validity.
	Natural experiments can be difficult to replicate with a different group of participants.

Experimental design

Independent groups: in an experiment with an independent groups design, different participants are used in each of the conditions.

Table 4.4 Strengths and weaknesses of independent groups design

Strength	Weakness
No participants are 'lost' between trials. Participants can be randomly allocated between the conditions to distribute individual differences evenly. There are no practice effects.	Needs more participants and there may be important differences between the groups to start with that are not removed by the random allocation of participants between conditions.

Repeated measures: in an experiment with a repeated measures design, the same participants are used in each of the conditions.

Table 4.5 Strengths and weaknesses of repeated measures design

Strength	Weakness
Requires fewer participants and controls for individual differences between participants as, in effect, the participants are compared against themselves.	It cannot be used in studies in which participation in one condition will affect responses in another (for example, where participants learn tasks). It cannot be used in studies where an order effect would create a problem (see below).

Matched pairs (matched participants): in an experiment with a matched pairs design, participants in each group are matched on a one-to-one basis on characteristics such as age or sex to control for the effect of individual differences.

Table 4.6 Strengths and weaknesses of matched pairs design

Strength	Weakness
Matching participants controls for some individual differences. It can be used when a repeated measures design is not appropriate (for example, when performing the task twice would result in a practice effect).	A large number of prospective participants is needed from which to select matched pairs. It is difficult to match on some characteristics (such as personality).

Interviews

One way to find out about people's behaviour is to ask them, and psychologists often do this. However, what we say about our behaviour and how we actually behave may be different.

In **structured interviews**, all participants are asked the same questions in the same order. In **unstructured interviews** participants can discuss anything freely and the interviewer can devise new questions on the basis of answers given previously.

Questionnaires

Questionnaires are usually written, but can be conducted face to face, or completed over the telephone, or on the internet. Printed questionnaires are completed by participants and are similar to structured interviews in that all participants are asked the same questions in the same order. Questionnaires are a practical way to collect a large amount of information quickly and they can be replicated.

> **Typical mistake**
>
> Telling the examiner that an advantage of using questionnaires is that they are 'quick, cheap and easy'!

Table 4.7 Strengths and weaknesses of interviews and questionnaires

Strength	Weakness
Questionnaires can be used with large samples of participants.	Self-report techniques cannot assume that participants will tell the truth; bias such as social desirability bias may lead to invalid results.
Structured interviews and questionnaires allow research to be replicated to test reliability.	Questionnaires or interviews may include leading questions that cause response bias.
Interviews allow rich detailed information to be gathered 'first hand' directly from the participants.	When closed questions are used, participants cannot explain their answers.

Case studies

A case study is a very detailed study into the life and background of one person (or of a small group of people). Case studies involve looking at past records and asking other people about the participant's past and present behaviour. They are often done on people who have unusual abilities or difficulties.

Table 4.8 Strengths and weaknesses of case studies

Strength	Weakness
They give a detailed picture of an individual and help to discover how a person's past may be related to their present behaviour.	They can only tell you about one person, so findings can never be generalised.
They can form a basis for future research.	The interviewer may be biased, and/or the interviewee may not tell the truth.
	Case studies may rely on memory, which may be inaccurate or distorted.

Observation studies

When psychologists conduct an observation, they usually watch people's behaviour but remain inconspicuous and do nothing to change or interfere with it. The following types of observations can be carried out:

- **Naturalistic observation:** people or animals are observed in their natural environment, without any sort of intervention or manipulation of behaviour.
- **Controlled observation:** the researcher may manipulate the behaviour of the observers or the observed.
- **Overt observation:** participants know they are being observed. This reduces ethical issues of consent and privacy but reduces validity due to increased demand characteristics.
- **Covert observation:** participants are unaware of the observation. This raises ethical issues (privacy and consent) but increases validity by reducing demand characteristics.
- **Participant observation:** the researchers get involved with the group of participants they are observing.

If several observers are coding behaviour in an observational study, **inter-observer reliability** assesses whether their coding or rating agrees with each other. To improve reliability, all observers must have clear and operationalised categories of behaviour and must be trained in how to use the system. Inter-observer reliability can be measured using correlational analysis, in which a high positive correlation among ratings indicates that high inter-observer reliability has been established.

> **Typical mistake**
> Telling the examiner that all covert observations are unethical.

Table 4.9 Strengths and weaknesses of observation studies

Strength	Weakness
Behaviour can be observed in its usual setting.	No explanation for the observed behaviour is gained because the observer counts instances of behaviour but does not ask participants to explain why they acted as they did.
Useful when researching children or animals.	Observers may 'see what they expect to see' (observer bias) or may miss or misinterpret behaviour.
A useful way to gather data for a pilot study.	Observation studies are difficult to replicate.

> **Revision activity**
> Make a wall chart grid showing each of the research methods and the main advantage and disadvantage of each method.

Correlation

Correlation is a statistical technique used to quantify the strength of relationship between two variables. Studies that use correlational analysis cannot draw conclusions about cause and effect. Just because two events occur together does not mean that one necessarily causes the other. Correlational data can be plotted as points on a scatter diagram (see Figure 4.1). A line of best fit is then drawn through the points to show the trend of the data.

- If both variables increase together, this is a **positive correlation**.
- If one variable increases as the other decreases, this is a **negative correlation**.
- If no line of best fit can be drawn, there is **no correlation**.

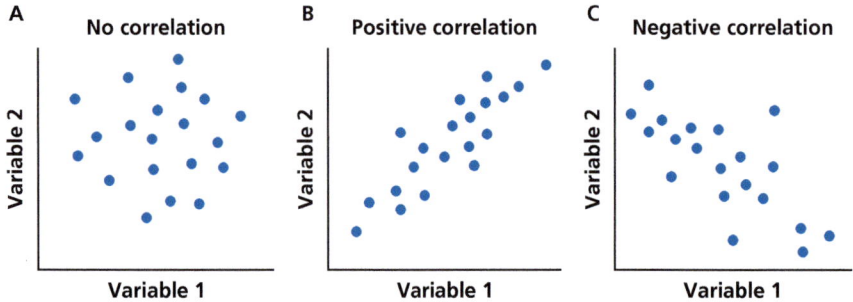

Figure 4.1 Scatter diagrams representing different types of correlation

Table 4.10 Strengths and weaknesses of correlational analysis

Strength	Weakness
Correlational analysis allows researchers to calculate the strength of a relationship between variables as a quantitative measure.	Researchers cannot assume that one variable causes the other.
Where a correlation is found, it is possible to make predictions about one variable from the other.	Correlation between variables may be misleading and can be misinterpreted.
A useful way to gather data for a pilot study.	A lack of correlation may not mean there is no relationship, because the relationship could be non-linear.

Revision activity

Sketch three scatter diagrams, one showing a positive correlation, one showing a negative correlation and one showing no correlation.

Now test yourself

1 What is a null hypothesis?
  A   A prediction ☐
  B   A prediction that the IV will have no effect ☐
  C   A prediction that the IV will have an effect ☐
  D   A prediction that the IV will have an opposite effect ☐
2 Which of these does a researcher manipulate?
  A   An extraneous variable ☐
  B   An independent variable ☐
  C   A dependent variable ☐
  D   A controlled variable ☐

→

3 Which of these describes a covert observation?
  A The observer is also a participant ☐
  B The observer is not a participant ☐
  C The participants do not know they are being observed ☐
  D The participants know they are being observed ☐
4 Which of the following is a weakness of using an interview to gain data?
  A Can only gain qualitative data ☐
  B Can't compare the answers given by participants ☐
  C Can only be used with small samples ☐
  D Low levels of validity because participants may not give true answers ☐
5 (a) *Eating chocolate has no effect on student cheerfulness.* Is this a null hypothesis or an alternative hypothesis?
  (b) Outline the main difference between a laboratory and a field experiment.
  (c) Outline one advantage of using an experimental method in psychological research.
  (d) Outline one disadvantage of using an experimental method in psychological research.
  (e) Outline one disadvantage of naturalistic observations.
  (f) Outline one advantage of using questionnaires to collect information.
  (g) Outline one disadvantage of using questionnaires to collect information.
  (h) What is the independent variable (IV) in a psychological experiment?
  (i) What is the dependent variable (DV) in a psychological experiment?
  (j) What is one advantage of using the observational method?
  (k) What is one disadvantage of carrying out an overt observation?
  (l) Why can't the findings from a case study be generalised to a wider population?
  (m) I approached people in my local town and asked them to complete a questionnaire on happiness. Was this a random sample of participants?

Answers on pp.102–3

Research procedures

REVISED ☐

Operationalisation of variables means being able to define variables in order to manipulate the IV and measure the DV. Both the IV and the DV need to be precisely operationalised otherwise the research cannot be replicated because another researcher would not be able to set up a study to repeat the same measurements.

Standardised procedures are what the researcher uses to reduce the chances of bias occurring. Standardised procedures may include:
- **Random allocation** in which participants in an independent groups design experiment are randomly allocated to determine which experimental condition they will take part in
- **Standardised instructions** which are usually written and will explain exactly what is required of the participant. Each participant should receive the same instructions. The briefing will tell the potential participant what the experiment is about, how the information will be used, and so on.
- A **debriefing** which takes place at the end of the experiment. Participants may be given an explanation of what they have just done and an opportunity to withdraw their data.

Counterbalancing

When a repeated measures design is used, problems may arise from participants doing the same task twice. When they carry out the task a second time, they may be better than the first time because they have had practice, or worse than the first time because they have lost interest or are tired. If this happens, then an **order effect** is occurring.

One way that researchers control for order effects is to use a **counterbalancing technique**. The group of participants is split, and half the group complete condition A followed by condition B; the other half completes condition B followed by condition A. In this way, any order effects are balanced out.

Extraneous variables are variables, other than the IV, that change between the conditions and are difficult to control (for example, how tired the participants are). Environmental variables that may affect participants' performance, such as the time of day or location, also need to be controlled.

Controls should be used to try to avoid variables, other than the IV, from affecting the DV. Controls can include random allocation of participants to experimental conditions to distribute individual differences within the sample equally between conditions. Controls can also include **counterbalancing** and the use of standardised instructions and procedures by which all participants are told what to do and are treated in exactly the same way.

Planning and conducting research

REVISED

Reliability and validity

Research should take into consideration the **reliability** and/or **validity** of the results. Reliability of results means consistency; in other words, if something is measured more than once, the same effect should result. If my tape measure tells me I am 152 cm tall one day but 182 cm tall the next, the tape measure I am using is not reliable.

Internal reliability refers to how consistently a method measures within itself. For example, my tape measure should measure the same distance between 0 cm and 10 cm as it does between 10 cm and 20 cm.

External reliability refers to the consistency of measures over time (that is, if repeated). For example, personality tests should not give different results if the same person is tested more than once.

Internal validity refers to the extent to which a measurement technique measures what it is supposed to measure, whether the IV really caused the effect on the DV or whether some other factor was responsible. Internal validity can be improved by controlling extraneous variables, using standardised instructions, counterbalancing, and eliminating demand characteristics and investigator effects.

External validity refers to the validity of a study outside the research situation and provides some idea of the extent to which the findings can be generalised. To assess the external validity of research, three factors should be considered:
1 How representative is the sample of participants of the population to which the results are to be generalised?
2 Do the research setting and situation generalise to a realistic real-life setting or situation?
3 Do the findings generalise to the past and to the future? For example, 50 years ago in the UK people were more conformist and obedient.

Face validity is simply whether the test appears, at face value, to measure what it claims to.

Improving validity

Internal validity can be improved by controlling extraneous variables, using standardised instructions, counter balancing, and eliminating demand characteristics and investigator effects.

External validity can be improved by setting experiments in an everyday, non-artificial setting, carrying out covert, rather than overt observations, and using random sampling techniques to select participants.

Demand characteristics and investigator effects

As soon as people know their behaviour is of interest, it is likely to change. Some ways in which participation in research can affect behaviour are:

- **Demand characteristics:** sometimes, features of the research situation may give cues to participants as to how they are expected to behave. This may lead to response bias, in which participants try to please the experimenter, so conclusions drawn from the findings may be invalid.
- **Social desirability bias:** people usually try to show themselves in the best possible way. So, when answering questions in interviews or questionnaires, they may give answers that are socially acceptable but not truthful. For example, people tend to under-report antisocial behaviour, such as alcohol consumption and smoking, and over-report prosocial behaviour, such as giving to charity.

Ethical considerations

REVISED

The British Psychological Society (BPS) has issued a set of ethical guidelines for research involving human participants. These ethical guidelines are designed to protect the wellbeing and dignity of research participants. The following guidelines are adapted from 'Ethical principles for conducting research with human participants'. The complete text is available on the British Psychological Society website (www.bps.org.uk).

Introduction

Good psychological research is possible only if there is mutual respect and confidence between investigators and participants. Ethical guidelines are necessary to clarify the conditions under which psychological research is acceptable.

The British Psychological Society
Promoting excellence in psychology

General

It is essential that the investigation should be considered from the standpoint of all participants; and foreseeable threats to their psychological wellbeing, health, values or dignity should be eliminated.

Consent

Whenever possible, the investigator should inform all participants of the objectives of the investigation. The investigator should inform the participants of all aspects of the research or intervention that might reasonably be expected to influence willingness to participate. Where research involves any persons under 16 years of age, consent should be obtained from parents or from those *in loco parentis*.

Deception

The misleading of participants is unacceptable if the participants are typically likely to object or show unease once debriefed. Intentional deception of the participants over the purpose and general nature of the investigation should be avoided whenever possible.

Debriefing

Where the participants are aware that they have taken part in an investigation, when the data have been collected the investigator should provide the participants with any necessary information to complete their understanding of the nature of the research.

Withdrawal from the investigation

At the onset of the investigation, investigators should make plain to participants their right to withdraw from the research at any time. The participant has the right to withdraw retrospectively any consent given, and to require that their own data, including recordings, be destroyed.

Confidentiality

Participants in psychological research have a right to expect that information they provide will be treated confidentially and, if published, will not be identifiable as theirs.

Protection of participants

Investigators have a responsibility to protect participants from physical and mental harm during the investigation. Normally, the risk of harm must be no greater than in ordinary life. Participants must be protected from stress by all appropriate measures, including the assurance that answers to personal questions need not be given.

Observational research

Studies based upon observation must respect the privacy and psychological wellbeing of the individuals studied. Unless those observed give their consent to being observed, observational research is only acceptable in situations where those observed would expect to be observed by strangers.

Giving advice

If a participant asks for advice concerning educational, personality, behavioural or health issues, caution should be exercised. If the issue is serious and the investigator is not qualified to offer assistance, the appropriate source of professional advice should be recommended.

> **Typical mistake**
>
> Not realising that debriefing a participant takes place *after* he or she has participated not before.

The dilemma for researchers is to design research that accurately portrays human behaviour while at the same time ensuring that they do not breach the ethical guidelines. In some situations where deception may be used, and it is not possible to obtain fully informed consent from the participants, psychologists propose the following alternatives.

Presumptive consent

This involves informing the people who are to be studied of the details of the study and asking them whether, if they were to participate, they would consider the research acceptable.

Prior general consent

This involves asking questions of people who have volunteered to participate before they are selected to take part. For example:
- Would you mind being involved in a study in which you were deceived?
- Would you mind taking part in a study if you were not informed of its true objectives?
- Would you mind taking part in a study that might cause you some stress?

> **Typical mistake**
>
> Failing to gain informed consent is *not* the same as deception. Make sure you understand the difference.

Participants who say they would not mind may later be selected to participate and it is assumed they have agreed in principle to the conditions of the study.

Research methods and ethical issues

Each research method raises different ethical issues:

- **Laboratory experiment:** even when told they have the right to withdraw, participants may feel reluctant to do so and may feel they should do things they would not normally do.
- **Field experiment:** it may be difficult to obtain informed consent and participants may not be able to withdraw. It may be difficult to debrief the participants.
- **Natural experiment:** confidentiality may be a problem, as the sample studied may be identifiable. Where naturally-occurring social variables are studied (for example, family income, ethnicity), ethical issues may arise when drawing conclusions and publishing the findings.
- **Correlational studies:** ethical issues can arise when researching relationships between socially sensitive variables because published results can be misinterpreted as suggesting 'cause and effect'.
- **Naturalistic observations:** if informed consent is not gained, people should only be observed in public places and where they would not be distressed to find they were being observed. If the location in which behaviour was observed is identifiable, an ethical issue may arise in terms of protecting confidentiality.
- **Interviews and questionnaires:** participants should not be asked embarrassing questions and should be reminded that they do not have to answer any questions if they do not wish to. Protecting confidentiality is important.

Now test yourself

TESTED

6 (a) A psychologist investigating mindset and learning styles designs a questionnaire to be circulated to all students. Identify one ethical issue the psychologist would need to consider.

(b) Students who revise for two hours a day for three weeks before the exam will attain higher grades in their maths exam than students who do not revise. Is this a null hypothesis or an alternative hypothesis?

7 (a) There are 53 students studying psychology. Explain how a researcher could obtain a random sample of 20 psychology students.

(b) Why is an opportunity sample almost always a biased sample?

(c) If you want a systematic sample of 20 from a list of 100 names, which names will you pick?

(d) Explain the difference between an independent groups design and a repeated measures design.

(e) You are going to conduct an observation of prosocial (helpful) behaviour on the high street. Suggest two categories of behaviour you might observe.

Answers on p.103

Quantitative and qualitative data

Experimental research, observations, interviews and questionnaires can result in quantitative and/or qualitative data.

Table 4.11 Strengths and weaknesses of quantitative and qualitative data

	Strength	Weakness
Quantitative data	<ul><li>Data is scientific and objective.</li><li>Numeric measures are used and data can be statistically analysed.</li><li>Data is high in reliability.</li></ul>	<ul><li>Data may lack detail.</li><li>Data often collected in contrived settings.</li></ul>
Qualitative data	<ul><li>Data is rich and detailed.</li><li>Data is often collected in real-life settings.</li><li>Data can provide information on people's attitudes, opinions and beliefs.</li></ul>	<ul><li>Data may be subjective and an imprecise measure.</li><li>Data may be low in reliability.</li></ul>

Revision activity

Make a list of two research studies that collected quantitative data and two research studies that collected qualitative data.

Primary and secondary data

Primary data is data that is collected by different methods, including observation, surveys, interviews, experiments and case studies. Primary data is more reliable than secondary data because the researcher knows its sources.

Secondary data is data that is collected from external sources, for example radio, internet, magazines, newspapers, reviews and research articles. However, with secondary data, issues such as validity and reliability occur as the researcher can be less sure of the accuracy of the source.

Computation

Decimals

A **decimal** is any number in our base-10 number system. A base number is the basis of a place value number system, in which successive powers of the base number are used for each column. The decimal system uses 10 as its base number so it is called a base-10 system. The decimal point is used to separate the ones place from the tenths place in decimals. (It is also used to separate pounds from pence in money.) As we move to the right of the decimal point, each number place is divided by 10 (see Table 4.12).

> **Decimal:** a number in our base-10 number system.

Table 4.12 Place value and decimals

Millions	Hundred thousands	Ten thousands	Thousands	Hundreds	Tens	Ones	And/Decimal point	Tenths, $\frac{1}{10}$	Hundredths, $\frac{1}{100}$	Thousandths, $\frac{1}{1000}$	Ten-thousandths, $\frac{1}{10000}$	Hundred-thousandths, $\frac{1}{100000}$	Millionths, $\frac{1}{1000000}$

For example, thousands divided by 10 gives you hundreds. This is also true for digits to the right of the decimal point. For example, tenths divided by 10 gives you hundredths. Thus, we read the decimal 59.46 as 'fifty-nine and forty-six hundredths'. Note that we usually read the decimal point as 'point' so, 59.46 would be read as 'fifty-nine point four six'.

Table 4.13 shows that each phrase can be written as a fraction and as a decimal.

Table 4.13 Phrases, fractions and decimals

Phrase	Fraction	Decimal
Six tenths	$\frac{6}{10}$	0.6
Seven hundredths	$\frac{7}{100}$	0.07
Fifty-two hundredths	$\frac{52}{100}$	0.52
Three hundred and eighty-seven thousandths	$\frac{387}{1000}$	0.387

Decimals are used in calculations that require more precision than whole numbers can provide. We use decimals to write three and one tenth of a pound of money as £3.10.

A decimal may have both a whole-number part and a fractional part. The whole-number part of a decimal is those digits to the left of the decimal point. The fractional part of a decimal is represented by the digits to the right of the decimal point.

Standard form

Standard form is a way of writing very large or very small numbers easily. They are written as a calculation which multiplies a number between 1 and 10 by the appropriate power of 10 to make that number.

For example: $10^3 = 1000$, so $4 \times 10^3 = 4000$. So, 4000 can be written as 4×10^3. It is useful to be able to write very large numbers in standard form.

> **Standard form:** a way of writing very large or very small numbers easily.

Small numbers can also be written in standard form. However, instead of the index being positive (in the above example, the index is +3), it will be negative (as in 10^{-2}). (The index is the small number that is raised up.)

When writing a number in standard form:
- first you write a number between 1 and 10
- then you write $\times$ 10 (to the power of a number).

Example:

92,800,000,000,000 in standard form = 9.28×10^{13}

Ratios, fractions and percentages

Ratios

In mathematics, a **ratio** is a relationship between two numbers of the same kind. For example, objects, persons, students, fruits, and so on. The relationship is expressed as **a to b** or **a : b**, indicating how many times the first number **a** contains the second number **b**.

In simple terms, a ratio represents, for every amount of one thing, how much there is of another thing. Ratios are always written in the simplest form.

Examples:

1 If there are 8 apples and 2 bananas, the ratio of apples to bananas is 8 : 2 but because 8 can be divided by 2, and 2 can be divided by 2, the ratio can be simplified to 4 : 1.
 $8 \div 2 = 4$
 $2 \div 2 = 1$
 The ratio of bananas to apples is 2 : 8, which can be simplified to 1 : 4.
2 If there are 10 fruits (8 apples and 2 bananas), the ratio of apples to the total amount of fruit is 8 : 10, which can be simplified to 4 : 5.

 The 4 : 5 ratio can be converted to a **fraction** of $\frac{4}{5}$ to represent how much of the fruit is apples.

Fractions

Fractions are simple! If you eat $\frac{1}{4}$ of a cake, you have eaten 1 of 4 parts. If you eat $\frac{1}{2}$ bar of chocolate, you have eaten 1 of 2 parts. If you share your cake equally with seven friends, each of you has eaten $\frac{1}{8}$ or 1 of 8 parts.

Converting ratios to fractions

Examples:

1 An observer records that the ratio of black cars to red cars in a car park is 3 : 1 (3 black cars for 1 red car).
 3 'parts' + 1 'part' = 4 'parts'

 3 of the 4 parts or $\frac{3}{4}$ of the cars are black.

 1 of the 4 parts or $\frac{1}{4}$ of the cars are red.
2 A supermarket worker counts the loaves of bread on the shelf. 20 loaves are brown and 15 loaves are white. The ratio of brown loaves to white loaves is 20 : 15 which can be simplified to 4 : 3, so in total there are 7 'parts'.

 So, $\frac{4}{7}$ of the loaves are brown, and $\frac{3}{7}$ of the loaves are white.

Ratio: a relationship between two numbers of the same kind.

Fraction: a way of expressing numeric parts of a whole.

Percentages

You need to be able to calculate **percentages** (%). For example, if you are handing questionnaires to an opportunity sample for the purpose of a survey, you may want to calculate what percentage of participants are male or female.

What does per cent mean? When you say 'per cent', you are really saying 'per 100'. One per cent (1%) means 1 per 100, 4% means 4 per 100, 50% means 50 per hundred, and so on. If a bank offers a rate of 4% per year on a savings bond, it means that for every £100 saved they will pay £4 interest.

Converting fractions to percentages

Some fractions are easy to convert to percentages:

$\frac{1}{100}$ = 1 per hundred and is 1%

$\frac{1}{10}$ = 10 per hundred and is 10%

$\frac{1}{2}$ = 50 per hundred and is 50%

$\frac{1}{4}$ = 25 per hundred and is 25%

Some fractions are less easy to convert but there is a method to do the conversion. For example, to convert $\frac{4}{5}$ to a percentage:

- Step 1: divide the numerator (top) of the fraction by the denominator (bottom), so 4 divided by 5 = 0.80.
- Step 2: multiply the result of step 1 by 100 (move the decimal point two places to the right), so 0.80 × 100 = 80.
- Step 3: round the answer up if needed (usually to two decimal places).
- Step 4: Add the % sign so the fraction $\frac{4}{5}$ as a percentage is 80%.

Estimating results

Estimating is a useful tool in everyday life. Being able to estimate is especially useful in psychology, because there is not a lot of point carrying out complicated statistical analysis if there is little or no difference between the two (or more) sets of scores. Being able to have a quick look at a set of data and estimating results accurately can save a lot of time.

You can think of estimating as 'rounding down' or 'rounding up' and you can use significant figures to get an approximate answer to a problem. For example, you buy a birthday present costing £5.99 and then you spend £3.99 on coffee and cake. By rounding up to the nearest whole pound it's easy to estimate that you have spent nearly £10.

(£5.99 rounded up to £6) + (£3.99 rounded up to £4) = £10

You can round up (or down) all the numbers in a mathematics problem to the nearest whole number to make 'easier' numbers. It is usually possible to do this in your head!

Examples:
1 Estimate the result of 8.9 divided by 3.07.
Step 1: round up the numerator 8.9 to the nearest whole number so that the numerator is 9.
Step 2: round down the denominator to the nearest whole number so that the denominator is 3.
Step 3: $\frac{9}{3}$ = 3

> **Percentage:** a way of saying 'per hundred'.

> **Revision activity**
>
> Practise calculating ratios, fractions and percentages! For example, when you go shopping and see a sign saying '10% off', calculate in your head how much the price has been reduced by.

The accurate answer is 2.899 which rounded to two decimal places is 2.90, so this is a good estimate.

2 Estimate the result of 583.48 divided by 1.94.

Step 1: round up the numerator (583.48) to the nearest whole number so that the numerator is 600.

Step 2: round up the denominator (1.94) to the nearest whole number so that the denominator is 2.

Step 3: $\frac{600}{2} = 300$

The accurate answer is 300.763 which rounded to two decimal places is 300.76, so this is a good estimate.

Significant figures

= means 'is equal to'   > means 'is greater than'   < means 'is less than'

Psychologists usually show the data they have collected in tables and the data is shown to two or three **significant figures**. You need to be able to use an appropriate number of significant figures and/or be able to calculate significant figures.

> **Significant figures:** The digits of a number that carry meaning.

Significant figures in decimals

15.787 rounded to one decimal place (d.p.) is 15.8 because in 15.7**8**7 the 8 is > 5 so rounds up to .8.

3.533 rounded to one decimal place (d.p.) is 3.5 because in 3.5**3**3 the 3 is < 5 so rounds down to 3.5.

However, when numbers are tiny, for example 0.00534 and 0.00328, rounding to one decimal place is not useful.

For example, 0.00534 rounded to one decimal place is 0.00 and 0.00328 rounded to one decimal place is 0.00.

This is not very accurate as these two numbers, though small, are not the same! So, to find an approximate answer with small numbers you use significant figures.

Counting significant figures

Significant figures start at the first non-zero number, so you ignore the zeros at the front but not, of course, the zeroes between the significant figures!

Examples:
1 In 0.0093, the first significant figure is 9, the second significant figure is 3.
2 In 0.0892, the first significant figure is 8, the second significant figure is 9, the third significant figure is 2.
3 In 0.0706, the first significant figure is 7, the second significant figure is 0, the third significant figure is 6.

Rounding significant figures

To round to a specific number of significant figures (s.f.), you use a similar method for rounding to a specific number of decimal places. You look at the number *after* the one you are interested in to see whether it is greater or less than five. If the number is equal to or greater than five, then round up. If the number is less than five, then round down.

Examples:

1 Round 0.0824591 to three significant figures (s.f.). To round to three significant figures, look at the fourth significant figure. It is 5, so round up and the answer is 0.0825.

2 Round 0.5400205 to four significant figures (s.f.). To round to four significant figures, look at the fifth significant figure. It is 2, so round down and the answer is 0.5400. Note: even though 0.5400 is the same as 0.54, include the zeros to show that you have rounded to four significant figures.

Revision activity

Practise rounding significant figures!

Exam tip

In the exam, if you are asked to perform a calculation, always double check your answer!

Now test yourself

8 Which of these is the correct way to write 5000 in standard form?
- A 5×10^3 ☐
- B 5 × 1000 ☐
- C 5 × 104 ☐
- D 4000 + 1000 ☐

9 (a) There are 16 ducks and 4 swans on a pond. What is the ratio of ducks to swans?
- A 16 : 4 ☐
- B 8 : 2 ☐
- C 16 : 20 ☐
- D 4 : 1 ☐

  (b) What percentage of the birds on the pond are ducks?

  (c) What percentage of the birds on the pond are swans?

  (d) What fraction of the birds disappeared when two ducks and two swans flew away?

10 An observer recorded that the ratio of males to females watching a football match was 3 : 1 (3 males for every female). What fraction of the audience was male?

11 Of the 35 cakes in the bakery, 20 were chocolate. What is the ratio of chocolate to other flavour cakes?

12 Convert the following fractions to percentages.

(a) $\dfrac{2}{100}$

(b) $\dfrac{1}{10}$

(c) $\dfrac{5}{20}$

(d) $\dfrac{20}{100}$

13 You go out shopping and spend £3.99 on a train ticket, £4.99 on a gift for a friend and £2.85 on a cup of coffee. Which of these is the correct estimation of how much you spent?
- A (£3.99 rounded up to £4) + (£4.99 rounded up to £5) + (£2.85 rounded up to £3.00) = £12
- B (£3.99 rounded up to £4) + (£4.99 rounded up to £5) + (£2.85 rounded down to £2.00) = £11

14 Estimate the result of 585.48 divided by 1.94.

15 Circle the first significant figure in each of the following numbers.
- (a) 0.0085
- (b) 0.095
- (c) 0.755

16 Round 0.0824691 to three significant figures.

17 Round 0.6400205 to four significant figures.

18 Write each of the following numbers as three significant figures.
- (a) 12.855
- (b) 1.588
- (c) 12.587

Answers on pp.103–4

Descriptive statistics

Measures of **central tendency** and **dispersion** are used to summarise large amounts of data into average values, and to provide information on the variability or spread of the scores. There are three ways to calculate a measure of central tendency (the average) of a set of scores: the mean, the **median** and the **mode**.

> **Median:** the central score in a list of rank-ordered scores.
>
> **Mode:** the score that occurs most frequently in a set of scores.
>
> **Arithmetic mean:** achieved by totalling all scores and dividing by the number of scores.

Mean

To calculate the **arithmetic mean**, all the scores are added up and the total is divided by the number of the scores.

Example:

Take the following set of scores: 2, 3, 5, 7, 8, 9, 17, 21.

The mean of this set of scores is 72 divided by 8 = 9.

> The advantage of the mean is that it takes all the values from the raw scores into account.
>
> However, if there are unusual (extremely high or low) scores in the data set, the mean can be distorted.

Median

The median is the central score in a list of rank-ordered scores. In an odd number of scores, the median is the middle number. In an even-numbered set of scores, the median is the midpoint between the two middle scores.

Example:

Take the following set of scores: 2, 4, 6, 6, 7, 9, 12, 17, 18.

The median of this set of scores is 7.

The mean of this set of scores is 9 (81 divided by 9).

> The advantage of the median is that it is not affected by extreme scores.
>
> However, the median does not take account of the values of all of the scores and it can be misleading if used in small sets of scores.

Mode

The mode is the score that occurs most frequently in a set of scores.

Example:

Take the following set of scores: 4, 4, 4, 5, 5, 6, 10, 12, 13, 14.

The mode of this set of scores is 4 because it occurs three times.

The median of this set of scores is $\frac{(5 + 6)}{2} = 5.5$.

The mean is 7.7 (77 divided by 10).

This example shows that each of the measures of central tendency may describe the midpoint of a set of scores differently.

The mode tells us nothing about the value of the scores or the other scores and there may be more than one mode in a set of data.

Range

Range is a measure of dispersion and it tells us about the spread of the data.

To calculate the range of a set of scores, subtract the lowest score from the highest score.

Example:

The range of 4, 4, 4, 5, 5, 6, 10, 12, 13, 14 is 14 − 4 = 10.

Note: the range can also be calculated as highest score minus lowest score plus one.

The range is a useful measure because if our research has more than one condition, we can compare the range of the scores in each condition. A low range indicates consistency in participant scores and thus low levels of individual differences. A high range indicates variation in participant scores and thus high levels of participant differences.

The advantage of the range is that it is easy and quick to work out.

However, the range can be misleading when there are extremely high or low scores in a data set.

Range: a measure of dispersion (the spread) of data

Revision activity

Look at tables of data and practise calculating the mean, median and range. Always check your calculations!

Interpretation and display of quantitative data

REVISED

Information provided in graphs and charts makes it easier for others to understand the findings of research.

Bar charts

Bar charts are used when scores are in categories, when there is no fixed order for the items on the *x*-axis, or can be used to show a comparison of means for continuous data. The bar chart in Figure 4.2 shows the results of a survey of pet ownership in percentages. (It doesn't add up to 100 per cent because some families reported owning dogs, cats, rabbits and fish!) The bars in bar charts should be the same width but should not touch.

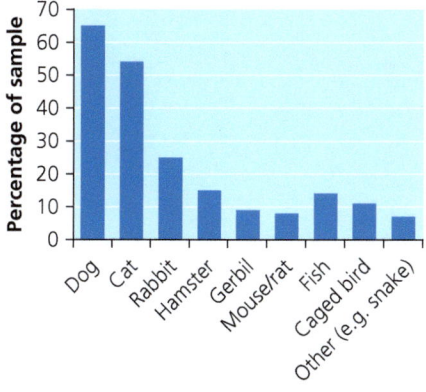

Figure 4.2 Bar chart showing pet ownership

Frequency tables

A frequency table is a table showing the values of one or more variables. The data collected during an observation is often collected on a frequency table. The tally chart example is a frequency table from an observation of car colours in a car park.

Table 4.14 Example of a frequency table

Colour of car	Tally	Frequency
red	IIIII IIIII I	11
green	IIIII III	8
silver	IIIII IIIII IIIII I	16
blue	IIIII I	6
black	III	3
white	IIIII IIIII II	12
other	IIII	4
total		60

Histograms

Histograms show frequencies of scores (how the scores are distributed) using columns. They should be used to display frequency **distributions of continuous data** and there should be no gaps between the bars. This example shows the test results (marks) for a class of students in a mock exam marked out of a maximum of 100. The test scores have been grouped into ranges of 10 marks.

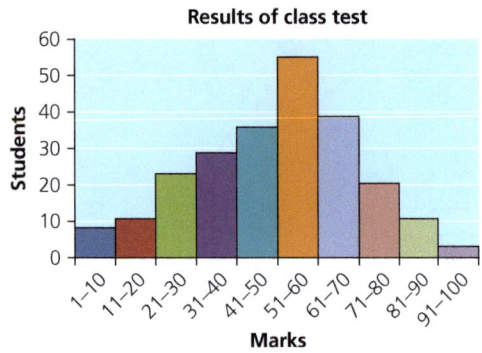

Figure 4.3 Histogram showing distribution of class test scores

> **Exam tip**
>
> Bar charts have gaps between the bars whereas histograms do not.

Scatter diagrams

Scatter diagrams are used to depict the result of correlational analysis. A scatter diagram shows at a glance whether there appears to be a positive or negative correlation, or no correlation.

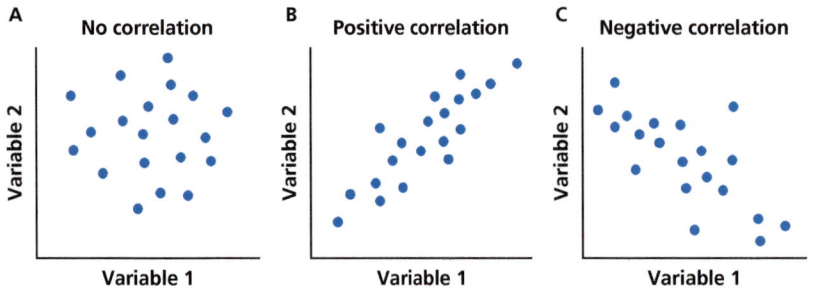

Figure 4.4 Scatter diagrams showing no correlation, positive correlation and negative correlation

> **Typical mistake**
>
> Forgetting to give a diagram a title and to label both the *x* and *y* axis.

Normal distributions

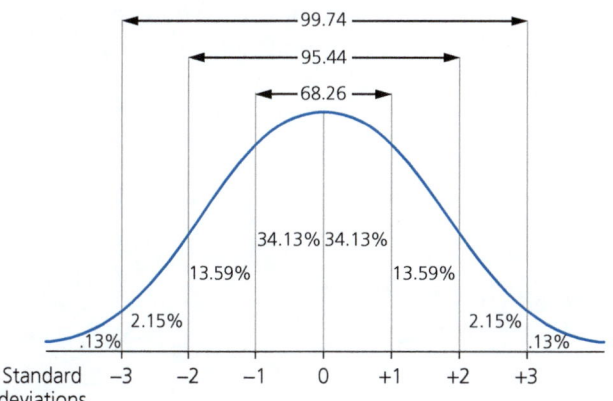

Figure 4.5 U-shaped curve of normal distribution

In a normally distributed set of scores:
- 68.26% of the scores lie +1 or −1 standard deviation above or below the mean
- 95.44% of the scores lie +2 or −2 standard deviations above or below the mean
- 99.74% of the scores lie +3 or −3 standard deviations above or below the mean.

Thus, in a normally distributed set of scores only 4.56% of the scores will lie more than +2 or −2 standard deviations above or below the mean.

Summary

For research methods, practical research skills, mathematical skills and data analysis and interpretation you should be able to demonstrate and apply knowledge and understanding of:

Formulation of testable hypotheses:
- Null hypothesis and alternative hypothesis.

Types of variable:
- Independent variable, dependent variable, extraneous variable.

Sampling methods:
- Target populations, samples and sampling methods
- Strengths and weaknesses of each sampling method
- Principles of sampling as applied to scientific data.

Designing research:
- Quantitative and qualitative methods
- Experimental method and experimental designs
- Laboratory, field and natural experiments
- Interviews, questionnaires and case studies
- Observation studies and interobserver reliability
- Strengths and weaknesses of each research method and types of research for which they are suitable.

Correlation:
- Association between two variables; scatter diagrams
- Strengths and weaknesses of correlations.

Research procedures:
- Standardised procedures, randomisation, counterbalancing.

Planning and conducting research:
- Reliability and validity
- Ethical issues
- Quantitative and qualitative data
- Primary and secondary data.

Computation:
- Decimal and standard form; ratios, fractions and percentages.

Descriptive statistics:
- Mean, median, mode and range.

Interpretation and display of quantitative data:
- Frequency tables and diagrams, bar charts, histograms and scatter diagrams.

Normal distributions:
- Characteristics of normal distributions.

Exam practice

1 A psychologist conducted a memory experiment by showing ten people a list of vehicle number plates for one minute and then asking them to write down as many of the number plates as they could remember.

In Condition A, participants saw the number plates written as:

A   PF5   83   YZ
B   CCA   68   9M
C   RFX   57   3W
D   YHZ   73   4B
E   UCA   61   2D.

In Condition B, participants saw the number plates written as:

A   PF583YZ
B   CCA689M
C   RFX573W
D   YHZ734B
E   UCA612D.

The psychologist recorded the number of correctly recalled letters and numbers in the right position in each number plate; for example, a score of six out of seven would be given if a participant wrote PF563YZ for (a). Each participant was given a total score. The maximum score was 35.

(a) Is this a laboratory or a natural experiment? [1 mark]
(b) What is the independent variable in this experiment? [1 mark]
(c) What is the dependent variable in this experiment? [1 mark]
(d) Write a null hypothesis for this experiment. [2 marks]

The results of the experiment are shown in Table 4.15.

Table 4.15 Memory experiment results

Participant	Condition A	Condition B
1	30	22
2	25	20
3	22	15
4	20	17
5	33	18
6	25	12
7	28	13
8	29	14
9	15	16
10	23	23
Total	250	170

(e) Calculate the mean memory score both for Condition A and for Condition B. Show your workings. [2 marks]
(f) The range for Condition A is 18 (33 minus 15). Calculate the range for Condition B. Show your working. [2 marks]
(g) From looking at the mean, what conclusion could the psychologist draw from this experiment? [3 marks]
(h) Looking at the range of the scores in Condition A and B, in which condition were the scores most consistent? [2 marks]
(i) The target population for this experiment on memory was university students. There were 200 students studying psychology at a local university. Describe how the psychologist could have used random sampling to select 20 participants. [3 marks]

➜

2 A teacher asked ten students to keep a diary for 14 days recording how long they spent on social media and how long they spent revising for their exams. This is what she found:

Table 4.16 Time spent on social media and time spent revising for exams

Participant	Hours on social media	Hours spent revising
1	1	17
2	15	6
3	13	8
4	5	16
5	9	10
6	20	2
7	7	12
8	11	9
9	16	4
10	6	14

(a) Draw a scatter diagram of the results shown in Table 4.16. Give it a suitable title and labels. [4 marks]

(b) Identify the type of correlation the teacher found. Shade one box only. [1 mark]

　　A　Negative correlation ☐
　　B　No correlation ☐
　　C　Perfect correlation ☐
　　D　Positive correlation ☐

(c) What could the teacher conclude from this data? Explain your answer. [3 marks]

Answers on pp.109–10

Exam tip

If you are asked to perform a calculation, always show your workings.

1 Social influence

Conformity

Social psychology focuses on how we interact with other people and how these interactions may influence our own behaviour. In this topic, you will learn how psychologists have defined social influence and why people conform. **Conformity** is the process of yielding (giving in) to majority influence. Myers (1999) referred to it as 'a change in behaviour due to real or imagined pressure' and Zimbardo (1995) described it as 'a tendency for people to adopt behaviour, attitudes and values of other members of a group'.

Conformity can be seen in many everyday situations, for example people may conform to a dress code at a party. Compliance occurs when a person conforms to the majority opinion but does not agree with it. If the group pressure is removed, conformity will cease. Compliance is thought to occur because some individual wishes to be accepted by the majority of the group.

Deutsch and Gerard (1955) suggested that there are two reasons why people conform:

- **Normative social influence** (social approval/the desire to be liked): this is the assumption that we conform because we prefer to be accepted by the group rather than to stand out (desire to be liked), possibly because it is advantageous for us to belong to a group.

Conformity: change in belief or behaviour.

Normative social influence: we conform through a desire to be liked.

- **Informational social influence** (information/the desire to be right): this is the assumption that we may conform if we are unsure of what to do or how to behave in an unfamiliar or ambiguous situation. We may look at other people for clues as to how to act and copy them as they may have more knowledge than us; we conform because we want to be right.

Social factors can affect conformity to majority influence

Social psychology argues that conformity is affected by the situation rather than the individual, in which case, if we manipulate the situation, we can change the conformity.

Asch carried out a laboratory experiment (see page 60) to show how he could manipulate the conformity levels of the participants. He went on to carry out a series of variations of the original study to identify the factors that influence conformity.

- **Group size:** this can affect conformity as individuals look to others and comply to fit in with the group norms as we have a desire to be liked.

In Asch's study, when there was one confederate, the real participants conformed on just three per cent of the critical trials. When the group size increased to two confederates, the real participants conformed on 12.8 per cent of the critical trials. When there were three confederates, the real participants conformed on 32 per cent of the critical trials, which was the same percentage as when there were seven confederates. This suggests that conformity reaches the highest level with just three confederates.

- **Anonymity:** during the studies carried out by Asch, the participants reported that one of the reasons they gave the incorrect answer was that they felt embarrassed to give the right answer. In this case where they 'privately' did not agree though they 'publicly' did, we could argue that they did not really conform. **Anonymity** affects conformity as when an individual is able to give their answers in private, they are less affected by group norms and less likely to conform.

Crutchfield carried out a study to observe the effect of majority influence on private conformity. The participants were placed in booths and asked to agree and disagree on a range of stimuli including the Asch-type perceptual judgement and were made aware of what they believed to be the answer of other participants (confederates). The level of conformity was 30 per cent, which was similar to Asch's original study.

- **Task difficulty:** one reason for conformity is when an individual is asked to perform a task that is unfamiliar and there is no clear answer. If the task is difficult and the individual is unsure of the correct answer, they will look to others for information as they have a desire to be right. In his variation, Asch adjusted the comparison lines to make them more similar to the standard line, making the difference between the line lengths significantly smaller and the task more difficult. In this variation Asch found the rate of conformity increased, probably because of informational social influence.

> **Exam tip**
>
> In the exam, you may have to explain a scenario using your knowledge of conformity. Make sure you find examples from the scenario and then link them to the explanation.

> **Informational social influence**: we conform through a desire to be right.
>
> **Anonymity**: an individual is able to stay unknown.

Dispositional factors can affect conformity to majority influence

Dispositional factors are related individual differences that exist between people and these can relate to our personality, how confident we feel at completing a task and our level of expertise.

From this viewpoint, the power of the individual is more influential than situational factors. This is clear from the results of Asch's study as 65 per cent of participants did not conform to social pressure and wanted to remain independent.

- **Personality** affects conformity as people with an external locus of control are more likely to conform because they do not believe themselves to control what happens to them or their lives. Therefore, they may not take responsibility for the things they do or consider the consequences of their actions and may be less independent.
- **Expertise** will also have an effect as the more confident we feel in a task, the less likely we are to conform. Expertise relates to how confident we feel at completing a specific task and whether we have the belief that we have the skill set to complete it. The greater the belief in our own ability, the less likely we are to conform to social pressure.

> **Revision activity**
>
> Make a mind map for all the factors that affect conformity. Use a different colour for each factor.

Key study: Asch's study of conformity

Aim: Solomon Asch conducted an experiment to investigate the extent to which social pressure from a majority group could affect a person to conform.

Method: Asch put a naive participant in a room with seven confederates. The confederates had agreed in advance what their responses would be when presented with the line task. The real participant did not know this and was led to believe that the other seven participants were also real participants like himself. Each person in the room had to state aloud which comparison line (A, B or C) was most like the target line. The answer was always obvious. The real participant sat at the end of the row and gave his answer last. In some trials, the seven confederates gave the wrong answer.

There were 18 trials in total and the confederates gave the wrong answer on 12 trials.

Results: Asch measured the number of times each participant conformed to the majority view. On average, about one third (32 per cent) of the participants in each trial went along and conformed with the clearly incorrect majority.

Three quarters of the participants (75 per cent) conformed on at least one trial.

Conclusion: When they were interviewed after the experiment, most of them said that they did not really believe their conforming answers but had gone along with the group for fear of being ridiculed or thought 'peculiar'. A few of them said that they really did believe the group's answers were correct.

Evaluation of Asch's study

Asch devised a situation in which it was easy to vary the amount of group pressure as he carried the study out in a laboratory setting and had high levels of control, improving the validity of the study.

The sample lacks generalisability as all participants were male students belonging to the same age group and it was therefore not representative of females or other age groups.

The study is low in ecological validity as the task (judging line lengths) was artificial as it is unlikely to happen in everyday life. Therefore, we cannot apply the findings to everyday life.

> **Exam tip**
>
> Asch is a key study, so you could be asked questions about the aim, method, results and conclusions as well as the ethics of the study.

Obedience

Obedience is following an order given by a person with recognised authority over you. Most of the time, this is a sensible thing to do, for example following orders given by a police officer or a teacher. However, obedience has sometimes been blamed for ordinary people committing horrible acts, for example Nazi soldiers following Hitler's orders.

Milgram's Agency theory

Obedience is a form of social influence that involves an authority figure passing instructions to an individual who will either obey or dissent.

- The agentic state is where we see ourselves as the agent or subordinate of a **legitimate authority**; we do not take responsibility for our actions as we believe ourselves to be acting on behalf of someone else, so they take blame or responsibility.
- The **autonomous** state is where we choose to voluntarily do something; we are aware of the consequences of our actions.

Milgram suggested that when given instructions by an authority figure, an individual sees themselves as an agent of the authority figure (that is, they act on their behalf). Many participants in his study experienced **moral strain** resulting in the individual becoming very uncomfortable and this can lead to high levels of anxiety. In order to reduce the anxiety, the individual will shift to the agentic state (**agentic shift**) relieving the moral strain as the responsibility for their actions is displaced onto the authority figure.

> **Obedience**: following the orders of a legitimate authority.
>
> **Legitimate authority**: a person we believe to be rightfully in charge.
>
> **Autonomous**: acting independently.
>
> **Moral strain**: anxiety experienced when ordered to do something against our will.
>
> **Agentic shift**: moving from the autonomous state to the agentic state.

Evaluation of Milgram's Agency theory

The theory is supported by research evidence; participants in Milgram's study (see below) were seen to be following orders and passed responsibility for their actions to the experimenter.

The theory can be applied to real-life events such as the torture of detainees by US soldiers in Abu Ghraib prison in Iraq and the behaviour of the Nazis during the Second World War. The soldiers saw themselves as agents for the person giving the orders.

Agency theory cannot explain individual differences in obedience. There were 35 per cent of participants in Milgram's study who dissented and did not go up to 450 volts.

> **Revision activity**
>
> Be creative and draw a storyboard to show how agency theory works in a real-life situation. For example, a security guard in a shopping centre asks you to drop some litter. Make sure you include all the stages.

Key study: Stanley Milgram (1974)

Stanley Milgram (1974) advertised for volunteers to take part in an experiment concerning memory and learning at Yale University. Forty men, aged between 20 and 50, volunteered.

When participants arrived, they were told that there would be two participants, a 'learner' and a 'teacher'. The experimenter drew lots to see which participant would take which part. The participant was not told the true details of the research.

The truth was that the other participant was in fact a confederate of the experimenter, and the 'experimenter' was also a confederate. The true

participant always ended up being given the role of the 'teacher'.

The 'teacher' was told to give electric shocks to the 'learner' every time the wrong answer was given, and the shock intensity was increased each time. In fact, the apparatus was arranged so that the learner never actually received any shocks. The maximum intensity of shock was 450 volts. If the teacher was unwilling to give shocks, the experimenter urged him to continue, saying such things as, 'It is absolutely essential that you should continue.'

The results were that 65 per cent of the participants continued to 450v.

Social factors affecting obedience

Social psychology would argue that situational factors influence obedience. Milgram demonstrated this as his research showed that 65 per cent of the participants were influenced by the authority figure rather than acting on their own individual morals.

- **Authority:** the authority figure has an influence on obedience as we are socialised to respect and obey authority figures such as teachers and the police. Obedience to authority is a necessary part of all democratic societies and enables us to live in harmony. The most important aspect of the importance of authority is the idea of a 'legitimate authority' – people we perceive to have legitimate reasons to make demands on us; for example, if the fire alarm goes off in a building, we would follow the instructions of the fire officers.

  Milgram showed the power of authority in his variation of his study where the role of the experimenter was played by an ordinary man. The change in the status of the authority figure resulted in the obedience levels falling to 20 per cent.

- **Culture:** there are two distinct types of culture – collectivist and individualistic.
  - ○ **Collectivist cultures** place an emphasis on the needs of the whole society rather than on themselves as individuals.
  - ○ **Individualistic cultures** place value on individual autonomy and priority of personal worth over the collective worth of the society.

  The UK and other Western countries, such as Europe and the USA, are seen as individualistic. Collectivist cultures include countries in the Far East, such as China and Japan.

  Smith and Bond (1998) found that people who belong to individualistic cultures, such as American and British cultures, are more likely to behave autonomously than those from collectivist cultures, such as Chinese and Japanese cultures. In collectivist cultures, group decision making is highly valued, but in individualistic cultures, people are more concerned with their independent success than the wellbeing of their community.

- **Proximity:** the proximity of the authority figure is an important factor in obedience and relates to the distance between the two.

  Milgram carried out a variation in his study where the experimenter started in the room and then left and gave instructions over the phone, and levels of obedience dropped from 65 per cent to 22.5 per cent. Milgram also looked at the proximity of the teacher and learner when they were seated in the same room. In this variation, the percentage of participants who administered the full 450 volts dropped from 65 per cent to 40 per cent. Obedience levels fell, as the teacher was able to experience the learner's pain more directly.

> **Proximity:** how close others are to us.

Dispositional factors affecting obedience: Adorno's theory of the Authoritarian Personality

Adorno proposed a theory that upbringing causes obedient personality traits. Adorno created the 'F' score (a measure of authoritarian personality) and set out to measure the extent to which children brought up by very strict parents grow up to be (as adults) more obedient and submissive to those in authority.

Milgram compared 'F' scores between obedient and disobedient participants and found higher 'F' scores in obedient participants. This suggests that, rather than the situation shaping our behaviour, obedience is linked to upbringing and personality.

There is research evidence to support the theory as Milgram and Elms compared the F scale scores for 20 obedient participants and 20 dissenters and found a higher level of authoritarian personality in the obedient participants.

The theory is based on correlational research between authoritarian personality and obedience and we cannot show that authoritarian personality causes obedience.

The theory uses a questionnaire which shows both strengths and weaknesses – we can access the participants' thoughts and feelings, but as Adorno's theory is based on past childhood experience, participants may not accurately recall or may give biased answers.

Revision activity

Make a mind map for all the factors affecting obedience. Use a different colour for each factor to help you remember them in the exam.

Exam tip

In the exam, you need to make it clear how the factors affect conformity and obedience. The best way to do this is to include an example.

Prosocial behaviour

REVISED

Prosocial behaviour is seen as behaviour that is of benefit to others, which may be at a cost to the individual. Prosocial behaviour includes empathy and helping. Antisocial behaviour is not a benefit to others and may include aggression and ignoring the plight of a person in need of help. This may include walking past people in the street who are in distress or have fallen or dropped their shopping. We have to decide if we will stop and help or carry on walking and ignore them. In many situations people become '**bystanders**' rather than help.

Social factors for helping

Bystander behaviour is of interest to social psychologists as they can explore reasons why people do and do not help when help is needed.

- **Presence of others**: the likelihood of us helping in an emergency situation diminishes proportionally by the number of people present. For example, if someone collapses in the street, we will not help if others are around, and the more people who are there, the less likely we are to help. This is known as the bystander effect.
- **Cost of helping:** one social factor influencing bystander behaviour is **cost–benefit analysis** where people will weigh up the cost to themselves in terms of time (if we are in a hurry or late for school), money (if we are wearing our best clothes) or risk to ourselves as the situation may place us in danger if we help. This is then compared to the benefits of helping in terms of positive feelings as a result of social approval and self-esteem.

Dispositional factors for helping

These also influence bystander intervention including:

- **Similarity to the victim:** we are more likely to help someone who is similar to us in terms of age, gender and race. This may be because we identify with them and therefore we empathise with them. Research has shown that we do not discriminate when helping a victim of another race if we are alone; however, if others are present from the same race as the victim, we are less likely to help.
- **Expertise:** this is another factor that influences bystander intervention. If we feel we do not have the necessary skills to help, such as being a first aider in a medical emergency, we may stand back and let others help.

Prosocial: acting in a way that benefits others rather than ourselves.

Bystander: a person who is present in an emergency situation but does not take part.

Presence of others: the effect of those around us.

Cost–benefit analysis: the trade-off being the cost to us and the benefit from our behaviour.

Revision activity

Look at the real-life murder of Kitty Genovese as an introduction to helping behaviour.

Revision activity

Highlight all the words you are not familiar with in this section and create a glossary.

Key study: Piliavin's subway study (1969)

Aim: To measure the effect of the type of victim on helping behaviour.

Method: A field experiment having an independent design and 103 trials over 2 months.

Sample: The participants were an opportunity sample of nearly 4500 passengers who happened to be on the New York subway (between 59th Street and 125th Street) on weekdays between 11 a.m. and 3 p.m. On average there were 43 people in the compartment in any one trial. Each trial lasted 7.5 minutes. On each trial, a team of 4 students boarded the train separately. Two female students acted as observers, one male student was a confederate (role model) and the other acted as a victim. There were four different teams, with a black 'victim' in one of the teams.

Procedure: There were two conditions used to test the hypothesis that 'people who are responsible for their own plight receive less help': the 'drunk' condition (the victim smells of alcohol and carries a bottle wrapped in a brown paper bag); and the cane condition (the victim is limping and carries a cane).

Seventy seconds after the train pulls out of the station, the male victim staggers and collapses. If no help is offered the role model steps in to help after either 70 seconds or 150 seconds. The point of this was to see if a 'model' (someone offering help) affected the behaviour of other passengers.

The two female observers recorded how long it took for passengers to help as well as information about the race, gender, and location of the passengers helped. The observers also noted what passengers said and who moved away in each condition.

Results: The cane victim received spontaneous help 95 per cent of the time (62/65 trials) whereas the drunk victim was spontaneously helped 50 per cent of the time (19/38 trials).

The cane victim was helped on average within 5 seconds, but the drunk victim was helped after 109 seconds. Only 24 per cent of drunk victims were helped before the role model stepped in, whereas 91 per cent of the cane victims were helped before the role model stepped in.

Neither white passengers nor black passengers were more helpful, but there was a slight 'same race' effect as white passengers were slightly more likely to help the 'white victim' than the 'black victim'. Eighty per cent of the first helpers were males. The more passengers there were near the victim the more likely help was given, thus there was no evidence of 'diffusion of responsibility'.

Conclusion: A two factor model (or theory) may explain why people help or do not help. **Factor 1:** An emergency situation creates a sense of empathy (arousal) in a bystander. This empathic arousal is increased if one feels a sense of identity with the victim, or if one is physically close to the victim. The arousal can be reduced by helping (directly or indirectly). It can also be reduced by going away or finding some way of rationalising why you can't help. **Factor 2:** Helping behaviour is determined by a cost-reward calculation, if the possible costs are greater than the possible rewards help is less likely.

Evaluation of Piliavin's study

A strength of the study is that it is high in ecological validity as it took place on the subway in New York, which is a real-life environment. Therefore, we can apply the findings beyond the setting of the study.

As the participants did not know they were being watched, their behaviour was natural, making the study more valid (few if any demand characteristics).

A weakness is that the study wasn't very reliable as it was difficult to control all the variables; for example, the researchers could not be sure if the passengers on the train were paying attention to the situation.

There are a number of ethical issues associated with the study; people did not know they were part of a study and therefore could not give consent, and they may have felt distress at seeing someone collapse on the train.

Revision activity

Use a cue card to summarise Piliavin's study. Include strengths and weaknesses.

Exam tip

You could be asked to design a study or think of different ways to measure bystander behaviour.

Crowd and collective behaviour

Prosocial and antisocial behaviour in crowds

Crowd behaviour can be prosocial or antisocial. Crowds at sporting events, such as the Olympic Games in London in 2012, can be peaceful and the collective group adds to the atmosphere in the stadium. However, there are also many examples of antisocial behaviour in groups, for example violence that accompanies some football matches. Examples of real-life **collective behaviour** can be explained in many ways including social factors that relate to the situation and dispositional factors that relate to the individual. If it is made clear to individuals that they are always responsible for their behaviour, then antisocial crowd behaviour can be reduced.

> **Collective behaviour**: the way people act when part of a group.
>
> **Social loafing**: the tendency for the motivation of members of a group to fall as the group size increases.
>
> **Deindividuation**: loss of autonomy as a result of being part of a group.

Social factors

- **Social loafing** is part of group behaviour and is based on research with tug of war teams where each individual who joined the team pulled less hard. Individual performance was reduced by 93 per cent in groups of two, 85 per cent in groups of four, and 49 per cent in groups of eight. Therefore, eight people only pulled the same as four people. However, when the participant becomes aware that their individual performance is identifiable, social loafing is eliminated.

- **Deindividuation** is the process by which individuals come to feel that they are part of a group or crowd, and so surrender their independence and autonomy. This tends to happen in large crowd situations where anonymity is possible, such as at a football match when fans are all wearing the same shirts, scarves and hats. Diener carried out a study where children were dressed in Halloween costumes and were allowed to take sweets from a bowl on the table. There was money near the bowl and the children in costumes stole the money. This is a way to explain antisocial behaviour in crowds. Individuated behaviour is rational, and consistent with personal norms, but in deindividuated behaviour people may act antisocially.

- **Culture** is a factor in collective behaviour as there are cultural differences in the norms and values that individuals live by. Collectivist cultures such as Japan and China are less affected by social loafing than individualistic cultures. In collectivist communities, the common goal for all is what is important for the group rather than the individual.

Dispositional factors

- **Personality:** one theory of personality is Rotter (1966). The idea of a 'locus of control' is an aspect of our personality that may lead us to act autonomously rather than just react to situational factors. Having an external locus of control means that you believe you have no control over the events that happen in life and that life events are controlled by external forces such as luck. An internal locus of control is the belief that you have control over the things that happen in your life. People with an external locus of control are less likely to take responsibility or consider the consequences of their actions. People with an internal locus of control are more likely to take responsibility and consider the consequences of their actions. In collective situations, people with an internal locus of control are less likely to follow the group.

- **Morality** is our sense of right and wrong based on the norms and values of our society and on an individual's ideas of what they believe to be just. The two may not always be the same and in some circumstances, we may believe it is right to 'stand up' against what we believe is unjust. The individual may defend their principles even if it means going against the rest of society and having to pay the consequences of social disapproval. For example, we may attend a march to protest for a cause or against an injustice.

Summary

You should now be able to demonstrate and apply knowledge and understanding of psychological ideas, processes, procedures and theories, and analyse and evaluate psychological ideas, information, processes and procedures in relation to:

Conformity:
- Social factors (group size, anonymity and task difficulty) and dispositional factors (personality, expertise) affecting conformity to majority influence
- Asch's study of conformity.

Obedience:
- Milgram's Agency theory of social factors affecting obedience including agency, authority, culture and proximity

- Adorno's theory of the Authoritarian Personality.

Prosocial behaviour:
- Bystander behaviour
- Social factors (presence of others and the cost of helping)
- Dispositional factors (similarity to victim and expertise)
- Piliavin's subway study.

Crowd and collective behaviour:
- Prosocial and antisocial behaviour in crowds
- Social factors (social loafing, deindividuation and culture)
- Dispositional factors (personality and morality).

Now test yourself

TESTED ☐

1 (a) 'A change in behaviour due to real or imagined pressure' is known as
    A Obedience ☐
    B Bystander behaviour ☐
    C Conformity ☐
    D Agency theory ☐

  (b) In Asch's study, what percentage of participants conformed on at least one trial?
    A 65% ☐
    B 32% ☐
    C 55% ☐
    D 75% ☐

  (c) If an individual chooses to voluntarily do something and is aware of the consequences of their actions, this is known as
    A Autonomous state ☐
    B Moral strain ☐
    C Agentic state ☐
    D Agentic shift ☐

2 (a) What is obedience?
  (b) Outline two social factors affecting conformity.
  (c) What is meant by 'moral strain'?
  (d) What is the role of moral strain in agency theory?
  (e) Outline Adorno's theory of the Authoritarian Personality.
  (f) What is collective behaviour?
  (g) Identify three recent real-life examples of collective behaviour.

➜

Exam tip

When answering questions that ask you to **identify** don't waste time writing long descriptions.

3 (a) When talking about antisocial behaviour, what is meant by 'deindividuation'?

(b) Katalina and Arti are with a group at school. The rest of the group have decided not to go to netball practice after school and they try to persuade the two girls not to go as well. Suggest one reason why Katalina might decide not to attend the training session and one reason why Arti might decide to attend.

(c) Explain how culture could influence prosocial and antisocial behaviour.

(d) Explain the difference between prosocial and antisocial behaviour.

4 (a) Explain the difference between an external locus of control and an internal locus of control in relation to prosocial behaviour.

(b) What was the aim of Piliavin's subway study?

(c) Who were the participants in Piliavin's subway study?

(d) Suggest one criticism of the research in Piliavin's subway study.

(e) Identify two factors that may influence bystander behaviour.

Answers on p.104

Exam tip

When answering a question that asks for an 'explanation' give an example to demonstrate your understanding.

Exam practice

1 (a) Identify **one** factor that has been shown to affect conformity. [1 mark]

(b) Use your knowledge of psychology to describe how the factor you have identified affects conformity. [3 marks]

2 Briefly discuss **two** criticisms of research into factors that affect conformity. [4 marks]

3 Camelia was on her way to work and had an important meeting to attend when she saw a young man fall over and graze his knees and cut his head. There were other people around and she was wearing her brand-new coat. Using your knowledge of bystander behaviour, explain why Camelia did not help. [3 marks]

4 Nancy is late for class and, as a short cut, decides to use the stairs in the school reception that has a no entry sign. As she reaches the top of the stairs, she notices one of the teachers is talking to the receptionist and changes her mind. Using what you know about obedience, outline why Nancy would obey the sign if a teacher is present. [2 marks]

5 Tia and Nick are talking about a football match where the crowds were behaving in an antisocial way. Identify one reason for the antisocial behaviour. [1 mark]

6 **Describe and evaluate** one study which investigated prosocial behaviour. In your answer include the aim of the study, the method used, the results obtained and the conclusion. [6 marks]

7 What is meant by the term 'Authoritarian Personality'? [2 marks]

8 Describe how having an authoritarian personality would affect your levels of obedience. [3 marks]

Answers on pp.110–11

Exam tip

Don't write several answers to a question that asks for just one answer. You won't get extra marks and you just waste time.

2 Language, thought and communication

> ## Key concepts
>
> Language and thought
>
> Piaget's theory: language depends on thought
>
> The Sapir–Whorf hypothesis: thinking depends on language
>
> Variation in recall of events and recognition of colours, e.g. in Native American cultures
>
> Limited functions of animal communication (survival, reproduction, territory, food)
>
> Von Frisch's bee study
>
> Properties of human communication not present in animal communication
>
> Definitions of non-verbal communication and verbal communication
>
> Functions of eye contact including regulating flow of conversation, signalling attraction and expressing emotion
>
> Body language including open and closed posture, postural echo and touch
>
> Personal space including cultural, status and gender differences
>
> Darwin's evolutionary theory of non-verbal communication as evolved and adaptive
>
> Evidence that non-verbal behaviour is innate, e.g. in neonates and the sensory deprived
>
> Evidence that non-verbal behaviour is learned
>
> Yuki's study of emoticons

Possible relationship between language and thought

REVISED

Piaget's theory: language depends on thought

Piaget proposed a theory that language is only acquired once a child has the cognitive ability, and language reflects thinking. He suggested there were four stages in cognitive development: sensorimotor (0 to 2 years), pre-operational (2 – 7 years), concrete operational (7 – 11 years) and formal operational (11+ years) and that thought was qualitatively different at each stage, which links to the sophistication of the language at each stage.

- **Sensorimotor stage:** a child's understanding of the world comes directly through their senses from moment to moment. The child thinks only about objects and/or people they can sense and/or manipulate, hence the term 'sensorimotor'. At this stage the child will tend to repeat sounds and words they hear from others.
- **Pre-operational stage:** the child is still dominated by the external world but is now able to create some simple internal representations of the world (schemas) through an increasing ability to use language. Piaget referred to the pre-operational child as **egocentric** and unable

> **Egocentric**: unable to view the world from the perspective of others.

to see things from other people's perspectives. Language at this stage reflects the child's tendency to focus on themselves and will include mostly verbalisations of what they are thinking and what they plan to do; they will tend to think out loud and read out loud rather than in their own heads.

- **Concrete operational stage:** the child is now able to conserve and can perform quite complex operations, but only if 'real' objects are 'at hand'. The child cannot perform mental operations (transformations) or hypothesise. In terms of language, the child will have a very wide vocabulary, though will be limited to only talking about concrete objects in the world.
- **Formal operational stage:** the child can now perform logical operations and abstract reasoning – but according to Piaget only 30 per cent of people ever achieve the stage of formal operations. During this stage the child is now able to discuss abstract ideas and hypothetical events.

Evaluation of Piaget's theory

One problem with Piaget's theory of language and thought is that it is based on limited evidence from observing his three children.

Piaget's theory was not tested experimentally as he used a series of observations and interviews with his own children. This makes his research biased as he could have used their responses to support his theory.

The Sapir–Whorf hypothesis can be used as an alternative explanation for the theory.

Sapir–Whorf hypothesis: thinking depends on language

The Sapir–Whorf hypothesis views the relationship between language and thought in an entirely reverse way to Piaget. In this theory, our thinking and the experience we have of the world is entirely based on our language. This suggests that culture has a significant impact on the way we think and the sense we make of the world. This concept is known as **linguistic determinism** as people who speak a different language will have a different perspective on the world – the language determines the thinking. Whorf's research showed that speakers of different kinds of language were, because of those language differences, cognitively different from one another.

> **Linguistic determinism**: language is affected by culture.

Whorf compared the language from different cultures and how the words they used were specific to the location as well as to the needs of the population. For example, the Hopi Indians in the US have one word to incorporate 'insect' and 'plane' as they have no need to show the difference between them, and the Inuits have many words to describe the different types of snow.

Evaluation of the Sapir–Whorf hypothesis

It could be argued that the Sapir–Whorf hypothesis presents a more plausible view of the relationship between language and thought.

There were flaws in Whorf's research as he did not actually research directly with the Hopi Indians and his research is seen as anecdotal rather than experimental.

Newstead (1995) suggested that Whorf was wrong to report that Inuits have 20 words for snow; in fact, they have relatively few words for snow and the same number as English speakers.

> **Revision activity**
>
> Make a table to show the differences between Piaget's theory of language and the Sapir–Whorf hypothesis.

Effect of language and thought on our view of the world

Variation in recall of events

Variation in recall is seen to be linked to culture and our experience of the world, and also links to schema theory. A study compared Spanish and English speakers and the difference in recall of accidental and intended events. There was a similar recall for the intentional event and a difference in the accidental event recall. This shows that the recall is relative to the language spoken. This concept is linked to schema theory in memory that suggests that recall will depend on our stored knowledge of what we expect to have happened rather than what actually happened. This can be linked to culture as our schemas are based on our cultural ideals. (Look back at Bartlett's 'War of the Ghosts', page 6.)

Colour recognition

According to the Sapir–Whorf hypothesis, the words we have for different colours affect the way we perceive or think about that colour.

> **Universalist**: language is universal.

Key study: Roberson *et al.* (2006)

Aim: To investigate the degree to which culture (through language) might influence thought.

Method: A study tracked colour naming and memory in two populations over three years. Roberson *et al.* (2006) compared young English children with children of the Himba tribe in Namibia. At the start of the study, the English children included 32 three year olds and 36 four year olds. The Himba children were 42 three year olds and 27 four year olds.

The study tested two hypotheses of colour categorisation:

- **Universalist** – that all humans categorise and remember colours the same way because we all share the same visual system
- Relativist – that colour perception depends upon culture and language.

The study observed how children learned colour categories and compared how the two groups of children mentally organised colour and named and comprehended words for colour. In the study, testers used sets of 22 coloured squares representing the English categories: the 11 basic terms of black, white, grey, red, green, blue, yellow, pink, orange, purple and brown, and 11 more colours halfway between the basic colours (for example, blue-green). Testers visited the children twice a year for three years and in each visit the children completed four tasks of listing colour terms, naming colours, comprehension and memory.

Results: Across both cultures the children acquired colour terms the same way, but over time, language had an increasing influence on how children categorised and remembered colours. The study showed that different languages have differing numbers of colour terms. English has 11 terms and Himba has five covering a broader range of colours. For example, the Himba tribe uses a collective term for the colours red, orange and pink. The findings show that for all the children their recognition of the colours was limited to the words they had learned for different colours.

Conclusion: The findings support the hypothesis that colour terms are learned relative to language and culture. For children who didn't know colour terms at the start of the study, the pattern of memory errors in both languages was very similar and the children didn't learn the primary colours of red, blue, green and yellow first. As both Himba and English children started learning their colour terms, the link between colour memory and colour language increased. The difference in colour perception suggests that cognitive colour categories are learned rather than innate.

> **Exam tip**
>
> Make sure you know the difference between the two theories in how they explain the link between language and thought.

Differences between human and animal communication

REVISED

Animals have the ability for **language** and **communication**, and we can communicate with each other using language, through written word, speech and gestures. Psychologists are interested in the way animals communicate and often make comparisons between human and animal communication. Although animals don't have language in the way humans do, they can communicate and in many ways are very impressive.

> **Language**: a way of communication in written, verbal or signing words that have meaning.
>
> **Communication**: a verbal or non-verbal way to send a message.

Limited functions of animal communication (survival, reproduction, territory, food)

In comparison to human communication, animal communication has limited functions. Non-human animals use language as a tool of survival, and communication is used in:

- Mate selection – for example male birds of paradise perform complex dances to attract females.
- Marking and defending territory – for example cats and dogs scent-mark boundaries of territory, and male dogs urinate on trees to communicate and mark their territory.
- Warning about danger – blackbirds call loudly, rapidly and repeatedly to communicate danger, rabbits thump their paws to warn other rabbits of possible predators.
- Finding food – food calls are used to inform the group that food has been found, and von Frisch (1993) reported that honey bees 'dance' to communicate a food location.

Key study: von Frisch's bee study

Von Frisch showed that honey bees use a dance language to communicate food locations to other bees. Once one honey bee finds a source of food, it returns to the hive to communicate the food location. Using the position of the sun, the bees 'dance' to communicate the location of the food. Von Frisch found two types of dance. The 'round dance' causes bees to look for food a short distance – up to about 50 metres – from the hive. The 'waggle dance' tells bees the direction and distance to fly to find more distant food sources.

The tempo of the dance tells recruits how far to fly; the slower the dance, the greater the distance of the food. The angle of the dance tells them the direction to fly and the dance lasts longer for more plentiful food sources.

Dances are also used when bees swarm, to help the swarm find a new home. When bees swarm, scouts dance to direct bees to potential nesting sites. After a number of bees have visited each possible nesting site, the best available location is chosen by having more bees dance for it.

Evaluation of von Frisch's bee study

Von Frisch won the Nobel Prize for his research on bees.

The study inspired other research to be carried out in animal communication and the original study has been replicated, increasing the validity.

However, later research with bees suggests that rather than communication, the bees have a cognitive ability for navigation.

> **Revision activity**
>
> Research von Frisch's study and draw some of the bee dances.

Properties of human communication not present in animal communication

It can be argued that in comparison to animal communication, humans have evolved to have far more sophisticated forms of communication. Table 6.1 shows the main differences between human and animal language and communication.

Table 6.1 Differences between human and animal language and communication

	Human	Animal
Duality of patterning	Sounds (phonemes) have no meaning but can be combined in an infinite number of ways to create words and meaning.	Animals do not communicate by arranging arbitrary sounds, which limits the number of messages they can create.
Creativity	New words can be invented easily.	Animals have to evolve in order for their signs to change.
Displacement	Humans can talk about things that aren't happening in their immediate environments (past, present and future) and human language can be used to plan future events.	Animal communication is immediate, context driven and is not used to communicate past events or plan for the future.
Interchangeability	Any gender can use the same language.	Some animal communications can only be used by one gender.
Arbitrariness	Human language is symbolic (words) which allows ideas to be recorded and preserved.	Animal communication is not symbolic, so it cannot be used to preserve ideas.
Biology	The human voice box and tongue are needed to generate the sounds of language.	Animals have different biological structures, which influence the sounds they make. e.g. birds 'sing', bees 'buzz'.
Ambiguity	A word can have several meanings.	A sign has one meaning.
Variety	Words can be combined to create an infinite number of ideas.	A limited number of combinations of sounds or movements can be used to communicate meaning.

> **Exam tip**
>
> This section contains some complex terms. Make sure you can explain them in your own words.

Non-verbal communication

Definitions of non-verbal communication and verbal communication

Communication is the intentional transmission of information from one person to another, which is understood by the person conveying the message and the person receiving the message. Verbal communication is sending a message through a spoken language that is understood by both the sender and receiver of the message. **Gestures** are a type of non-verbal communication that can be used to send a message.

- **Non-verbal communication** is communication that does not involve verbal or written communication and is also known as body language. Non-verbal communication includes gestures and facial expression.
- **Verbal communication** is the passing on of information using words through speech and written communication.

> **Gestures**: movements of the body to communicate with others.

Functions of eye contact including regulating flow of conversation, signalling attraction and expressing emotion

One function of eye contact is to regulate the flow of a conversation; the person speaking is watching the eyes of the listener for an indication that they are listening and about to interrupt, so the speaker knows when to stop talking and let the other person speak. The listener is watching the eyes of the person speaking to judge when they can interrupt, therefore eye contact regulates turn-taking in conversation. It feels very odd to hold a conversation with someone who is not making eye contact – a point to remember when you are tempted to check your phone!

Key study: Argyle (1975)

Aim: To see how interrupting eye contact affects conversation.

Method: Pairs of participants were observed (watched) having conversations. In half of the conversations, one participant wore dark glasses so that the other couldn't receive eye contact.

Results: When one of the participants wore dark glasses, there were more pauses and interruptions than when dark glasses were not worn.

Conclusion: Eye contact is important in ensuring the smooth flow of conversation.

Another function of eye contact is **signalling** attraction. Eye contact is a powerful signal – especially through the pupils as we respond to them as they dilate. When you meet someone for the first time, your eyes lock across the room; you look into the eyes of the person and if you find them attractive your pupils will dilate. This is an unconscious process and in turn they will respond to your dilated pupils as they will find it attractive.

> **Signalling**: a form of intentional communication including visual, auditory and touch.

Key study: Hess (1963)

Aim: To see the effect of pupil dilation on emotion.

Method: Participants were shown two sets of photographs of eyes. In one set, the pupils had been enlarged. In the other, the pupils had been reduced.

Results: Participants preferred the photos of the eyes with the enlarged pupils, mainly because they found them more attractive. They couldn't explain why.

Conclusion: Pupil dilation has an unconscious but powerful effect on emotion.

Expression of **emotions** is another function of eye contact. How we experience emotions when there is eye contact is different depending on whether the emotion is positive or negative. For example, if the emotion is positive, such as happiness, eye contact will make the emotion more positive, and if the emotion is negative, such as anger, then eye contact will make the experience of the emotion more negative.

Body language

Body language is the unconscious and conscious way we communicate our feelings to the outside world, and it can contradict what we are verbally communicating or match our communication. It is also known as kinesthetics and involves the actual movement of the body. Body language can draw attention and be used to enhance messages we wish to convey. One aspect of body language is the use of posture, which is how we position our body to strengthen our communication. Politicians will make changes in posture during speeches to make their point more convincing.

Posture is a non-verbal communication signal which involves the positioning of the body.
- **Closed posture** – positioning the arms so that they are folded across the body and/or crossing the legs.
- **Open posture** – positioning the arms so they are not folded across the body and not crossing the legs.
- **Postural echo** – this is where you mirror the body language of the person you are communicating with in order to put a person at ease.
- **Touch** – touch is part of body language and can put a person at ease, for example by touching the arm to reduce anxiety, though this needs to be used with care.

Personal space

How much space a person needs when in a social situation can be defined as 'an invisible bubble' surrounding that person into which others may not pass. It is the distance between ourselves and others that we feel comfortable with and can be measured as an exact distance. If people invade our personal space, we may feel uncomfortable and try to move away from them to regain the space required.
- **Culture and personal space:** research has shown there are cultural differences in how we perceive personal space, for example Argentinians have the smallest personal space from strangers and Romanians the largest.

> **Emotions**: feelings we experience, for example happiness, sadness, anger and surprise.

> **Revision activity**
>
> Have a look at all the emojis available. How much are the eyes part of how we convey emotions?

Key study: Summer (1969)

Aim: To see if there are cultural differences in the use of personal space.

Method: Summer observed groups of white English people and groups of Arab people in conversation.

Results: The comfortable conversation distance for the white English people was 1–1.5 m, whereas the comfortable conversation distance for the Arab people was much less.

Conclusion: The use of personal space in normal conversation varies with culture.

- **Status and personal space:** the larger amount of personal space required by people with a high status is shown by their larger homes and gardens, and so on. It is also suggested that our perception of personal space differs between those of similar status to us and those of a higher or lower status.

Key study: Zahn (1991)

Aim: To see if status influences personal space.

Method: Zahn observed people of equal status approaching each other to have a conversation. He also observed people of unequal status approaching each other.

Results: Zahn found that people of lower status did not approach higher-status people with the same degree of closeness as those of equal status.

Conclusion: The use of personal space varies with differences in status when approaching other people.

- **Gender and personal space:** there are also clear differences between gender groups in terms of personal space. Overall, females have a lower perceived personal space than males when in both same gender and different gender groups. The personal space between males is larger than between females.

Key study: Argyle and Dean (1965)

Aim: To see if there are gender differences that affect personal space.

Method: One at a time, participants were asked to sit and have a conversation with another person who was actually a confederate of the experimenter. Sometimes the confederate was the same sex as the participant and sometimes the confederate was of the opposite sex. The confederate sat at different distances from the participant and continually looked into the participant's eyes.

Results: The participants tended to break eye contact with the confederate of the opposite sex at a greater distance apart than when the confederate was of the same sex. Argyle and Dean thought that it was at this point that personal space was being invaded.

Conclusion: We prefer to have a greater amount of personal space between ourselves and members of the opposite sex during normal conversation.

Evaluation of personal space studies

Personal space can be measured in a reliable way as we can objectively measure the distance at which point an individual feels uncomfortable. This makes the research replicable.

There may be other variables that affect perceptions of personal space, such as past experience or how well we know or like the person.

Revision activity

Read the article www.independent.co.uk/life-style/personal-space-boundaries-different-countries-argentina-uk-romania-a7713051.html

Exam tip

You can use the studies to explain the differences relating to personal space. Ensure you are concise in your explanation.

Explanations of non-verbal behaviour

Darwin's evolutionary theory of non-verbal communication as evolved and adaptive

According to Darwin's theory, behaviour that is adaptive enables survival and is passed on through the generations. Darwin's theory is based mainly on physical characteristics, and **evolutionary** psychologists suggest that this is also the same for psychological behaviours such as non-verbal communication. Therefore, non-verbal communication may be a result of nature rather than nurture:

- Non-verbal communication designed to ensure **survival** includes warding off potential threats, reducing conflict and allowing cooperation between an individual and others.
- Non-verbal communication designed to enable **reproduction** involves flirting, appearing attractive to a possible mate and communicating in a relationship.

> **Evolutionary:** behaviour that is passed through the generations, is adaptive enabling survival.

Evaluation of Darwin's theory

Darwin's theory for physical characteristics is widely accepted as a theory; however this may not be the case for psychological behaviour such as non-verbal communication.

The theory is based on retrospective ideas; we have no way of going back into our past to test them.

The theory is just based on nature and ignores the influence of the environment; it may be an interaction of both.

There is evidence that nature has at least some influence on non-verbal communication as some gestures appear to be universal, for example smiling to show pleasure, blushing for embarrassment and crying to show distress.

> **Revision activity**
>
> Write down six to eight key words related to Darwin's theory of non-verbal communication and use these words to write a summary of the theory.

Evidence that non-verbal behaviour is innate

Generally, **innate** cues are universal and not linked to culture, for example smiling, crying and laughing. Therefore, there is an argument that non-verbal communication is innate and not learned.

One way to test this is to study the communication skills of babies (**neonates**) who are unable to use language and yet need to communicate with their caregivers in order to survive. Caregivers need to pick up on the non-verbal cues of the baby to know what they are feeling – for example, is the baby feeling hungry, wet, too cold or too warm? This would suggest that babies have an innate set of cues that they can use at the appropriate time. Non-verbal cues may include smiling or reaching towards their caregiver.

Another way to test the argument that non-verbal communication is innate is to study people who are sensory deprived. If children who are born blind are still able to use non-verbal cues such as smiling, this shows that the non-verbal cues are innate and not learned.

> **Innate:** behaviour that is present at birth (nature not nurture)
>
> **Neonate:** a very young baby.

Evidence that non-verbal behaviour is learned

Social learning theory starts with the idea that we observe and copy behaviours of the same species. Social learning theory argues that humans observe others; they pay attention consciously and unconsciously to the behaviour of role models around them. They then imitate those around them who they admire or love. If this behaviour is rewarded and reinforced, it is repeated, and the behaviour becomes habit. However, if this behaviour is criticised, it can stop us repeating the behaviour.

The social learning theory of non-verbal communication is supported by cultural variations in body language. Cultural variation can be observed in how people greet each other. In France, friends greet each other by kissing each cheek. In Brazil, the custom is to shake hands with everyone in a group, or for women to exchange kisses twice if they are married and three times if they are single. In Saudi Arabia, if you are a woman, no body contact is involved when meeting others. If non-verbal communication is not learned but innate, then humans would all communicate in more or less the same way.

Evaluation of social learning theory

Social learning theory of non-verbal communication suggests that people can learn new ways of communicating non-verbally, but this is not necessarily true. For example, efforts to teach offenders more appropriate body language tend not to be very effective.

Social learning theory cannot really explain why children brought up in the same environment can have quite different ways of communicating. For example, two brothers raised by the same parents in the same community can have very different ways of expressing themselves.

There is evidence that nature has at least some influence on non-verbal communication. Some gestures appear to be universal, for example smiling to show pleasure, blushing for embarrassment and crying to show distress. This would suggest that these examples are a product of nature and not nurture.

Key study: Yuki's study of emoticons

Aim: To investigate whether there are cultural differences in using the eyes and mouth as cues to recognise emotions in Japan and the United States.

Method: Yuki et al. carried out a cross-cultural study with 118 volunteer American students and 95 volunteer Japanese students. They completed a questionnaire where they were asked to rate on a scale of 1 (very sad) to 9 (very happy) the emotional expressions of six different emoticons with combinations of happy and sad eyes and mouths.

Results: The two cultures responded differently to the emoticons. The Japanese gave higher ratings to faces with happy eyes and the American participants gave higher ratings to faces with happy mouths. This shows that there are cultural differences in how emotions are expressed and interpreted in faces.

Conclusion: Overall this suggests that this aspect of non-verbal communication is affected by upbringing and cultural experiences.

Evaluation of Yuki's study

The research lacks ecological validity because emoticons are not the same as human faces.

Another criticism is that the sample was not very representative as it only represented one age group. Older or younger age groups may interpret faces differently.

The dependent variable was measured in a very simple way. Recognising emotions is a complex process and so just measuring it on a scale of 1 to 9 is not very reliable.

Exam tip

When evaluating a study in the exam, make sure you use examples to back up your points as it will make your answer more relevant.

Summary

You should now be able to demonstrate and apply knowledge and understanding of psychological ideas, processes, procedures and theories, and analyse and evaluate psychological ideas, information, processes and procedures in relation to:

The possible relationship between language and thought:
- Piaget's theory: language depends on thought
- The Sapir–Whorf hypothesis: thinking depends on language.

The effect of language and thought on our view of the world:
- Variation in recall of events and recognition of colours, e.g. in Native American cultures.

Differences between human and animal communication:
- Limited functions of animal communication (survival, reproduction, territory, food)
- Von Frisch's bee study

- Properties of human communication not present in animal communication, e.g. plan ahead and discuss future events.

Non-verbal communication:
- Definitions of non-verbal communication and verbal communication
- Functions of eye contact including regulating flow of conversation, signalling attraction and expressing emotion
- Body language including open and closed posture, postural echo and touch
- Personal space including cultural, status and gender differences.

Explanations of non-verbal behaviour:
- Darwin's evolutionary theory of non-verbal communication as evolved and adaptive
- Evidence that non-verbal behaviour is innate, e.g. in neonates and the sensory deprived
- Evidence that non-verbal behaviour is learned
- Yuki's study of emoticons.

Now test yourself

TESTED ☐

1 Which of the following is not a property of human communication but is found in animal communication?
   A Creativity ☐
   B Ambiguity ☐
   C Marking territory ☐
   D Duality of patterning ☐
2 Fill in the blanks.
   (a) _____ is also known as kinesthetics and involves the actual movement of the body.
   (b) In Piaget's theory of language and thought, at the _____ stage the child will tend to repeat sounds and words they hear from others.
   (c) The Sapir–Whorf hypothesis suggests that culture has a large impact on the way we think and the sense we make of the world. This concept is known as _____ _____ .
   (d) All humans categorise and remember colours the same way because we all share the same visual system. This is the _____ hypothesis.
   (e) Eyes are perceived as more attractive when the pupils are _____.
   (f) Words can be combined to create an infinite number of ideas. This is known as _____ .
   (g) _____ communication is the passing on of information using words; it can also include written communication.
   (h) _____ is the distance between ourselves and others that we feel comfortable with.
   (i) Describe the status differences in personal space.
3 Describe how non-verbal communication may be innate.
4 Explain the variation in recall of events.
5 Outline Piaget's theory of language.
6 Explain the function of eye contact in expressing emotions.
7 Outline Yuki's study of emoticons.
8 Evaluate Yuki's study of emoticons.
9 Outline evidence that non-verbal communication is innate.
10 Outline Darwin's evolutionary theory of non-verbal communication.

Answers on pp.104–5

Exam practice

1 Study Table 6.2 and apply what you know about culture and personal space to explain the findings. [3 marks]

Table 6.2 Average distance (in cm) for personal space from a stranger

	Distance (cm)
Argentinians	76
British	80

2 What term is used to describe when you mirror the posture of another person? Shade one box only. [1 mark]
   A Open ☐
   B Closed ☐
   C Postural echo ☐
   D Touch ☐

3 Evaluate von Frisch's bee study. [3 marks]

4 Describe **one** difference between open and closed posture in non-verbal communication. [3 marks]

5 Describe Piaget's theory of language and thought. [4 marks]

6 Use your knowledge of psychology to evaluate the Sapir–Whorf hypothesis that thinking depends on language. [5 marks]

7 Evaluate research into the variation in recognition of colours. [6 marks]

8 Outline **two** of the limited functions of animal communication. [4 marks]

9 Describe the function of eye contact in regulating flow of conversation. [3 marks]

10 Discuss evidence that non-verbal behaviour is learned. [6 marks]

Answers on p.111

3 Brain and neuropsychology

Key concepts

The divisions of the human nervous system: central and peripheral (somatic and autonomic)

The autonomic nervous system

The fight or flight response

The James–Lange theory of emotion

Sensory, relay and motor neurons

Synaptic transmission: release and reuptake of neurotransmitters

Excitation and inhibition

Hebb's theory of learning and neuronal growth

Brain structure: frontal lobe, temporal lobe, parietal lobe, occipital lobe and cerebellum

Basic function of these structures

Localisation of function in the brain: motor, somatosensory, visual, auditory and language areas

Penfield's study of the interpretive cortex

Cognitive neuroscience

Scanning techniques to identify brain functioning: CT, PET and fMRI scans

Tulving's 'gold' memory study

Neurological damage, e.g. stroke or injury, can affect motor abilities and behaviour

Structure and function of the nervous system

REVISED

Divisions of the human nervous system: central and peripheral

The nervous system is broken down into two major systems: the central nervous system and the peripheral nervous system.

The **central nervous system** consists of the brain and the spinal cord which act together. The brain stem is involved in life-sustaining functions and damage to the brain stem is often fatal. The brain stem includes the medulla oblongata, which controls heartbeat, breathing, blood pressure, digestion; the reticular activating system, involved in arousal, attention and sleep; and the cerebellum, involved in balance, smooth movement and posture.

The **peripheral nervous system** is divided into two sub-systems – the somatic nervous system, whose primary function is to regulate the actions of the skeletal muscles, and the **autonomic nervous system** (ANS), which regulates involuntary activity such as heart rate, breathing, blood pressure and digestion.

Central nervous system: the part of the nervous system consisting of the brain and spinal cord.

Peripheral nervous system: the part of the nervous system that is outside the central nervous system; it connects the CNS to the limbs and the organs.

Autonomic nervous system: the part of the nervous system responsible for control of bodily functions such as breathing, the heartbeat, and digestive process.

Quick quizzes at www.hoddereducation.co.uk/myrevisionnotesdownloads

Autonomic nervous system and the fight or flight response

The sympathetic nervous system is part of the autonomic nervous system and controls what has been called the **fight or flight** response.

In a fight or flight situation the sympathetic nervous system prepares the body: heart rate quickens to get more blood to the muscles; breathing becomes faster and deeper to increase oxygen; blood flow is diverted from the organs so digestion is reduced; and pupils dilate for better vision. In an instant, your body is prepared to either defend or escape.

The fight or flight response is a chain of rapidly occurring physiological reactions that mobilises the body's resources to deal with threatening circumstances. It originates in the hypothalamus and includes the pituitary and adrenal glands. This hypothalamic–pituitary–adrenal axis is responsible for arousing the ANS in response to a threat. The sympathetic branch of the nervous system stimulates the adrenal gland to release adrenaline, noradrenaline and corticosteroids into the bloodstream. The increase in adrenaline produces the physiological reactions, such as increased heart rate and blood pressure and a dry mouth, known as the fight or flight response. After the threat is gone, it takes 20 to 60 minutes for the body to return to its pre-arousal levels.

> **Fight or flight**: response of the nervous system to an emergency to prepare to run or stay and fight.

> **Revision activity**
>
> Write a set of quiz questions for the fight or flight response and test your friends.

James–Lange theory of emotion

The James–Lange theory of emotion suggests that we experience situations and events in the environment that lead to a change in our physiological reactions, such as increased heart rate, perspiration, dryness of the mouth, and others; these reactions are created by the autonomic nervous system. The theory suggests that emotions are a result of these physiological responses, and not their cause. The perception of emotion-arousing stimuli is followed by specific physiological reactions such as release of adrenaline and flight reaction. The brain interprets the specific physiological changes as the emotion, 'I'm scared because my heart is racing, and I am running away.'

Evaluation of James–Lange theory of emotion

Levenson *et al.* (1990) found that when participants were asked to make facial expressions for fear, anger, happiness, disgust, sadness and surprise, and to hold these expressions for ten seconds, there was slight change in heart rate, skin temperature, and other physiological reactions for the different emotions.

However, although there was a change, they were unable to detect which emotion was being experienced.

Maranon (1924) found that physiological arousal is not enough to cause emotion. Only around two-thirds of participants who were injected with adrenaline reported physical symptoms.

Schachter and Singer (1962) suggest that emotions are the result of not just physiological changes, but there is also a cognitive component as we interpret the situation.

> **Revision activity**
>
> Be creative and make a storyboard to explain the James–Lange theory of emotion and then do the same to show how Schachter and Singer's theory is different. You could relate it to a real-life situation, for example winning the lottery or waiting to go into an exam.

Neuron structure and function

Neurons are the basic building blocks of the nervous system. These specialised cells are the information-processing units of the brain responsible for receiving and transmitting information. Each part of the neuron plays a role in the communication of information throughout the body. There are three basic parts of a neuron: the **dendrites**, the cell body and the **axon**. However, all neurons vary somewhat in size, shape and characteristics depending on the function and role of the neuron. Some neurons have few dendritic branches, while others are highly branched in order to receive a great deal of information. Some neurons have short axons, while others can be quite long.

Sensory, relay and motor neurons

Sensory neurons are afferent neurons, meaning they relay information to the brain only. Relay and motor neurons can carry a message in one direction only. Motor neurons carry information from the brain to the target. **Relay neurons** carry information from sensory neurons to motor neurons, bypassing the brain; for example, if you touched a hot stove and the signal went all the way to your brain and back, your hand would be much more burned than if you instantly pulled it away from the stove.

Information comes to the neuron through the dendrites from other neurons and then continues to the cell body (soma), which is the main part of the neuron, containing the nucleus and maintaining the life-sustaining functions of the neuron. The soma processes information and then passes it along the axon. At the end of the axon are bulb-like structures called terminal buttons, which pass on the information to glands, muscles or other neurons.

Synaptic transmission: release and reuptake of neurotransmitters

Neurotransmitters are needed to send the information from one neuron to the next. Neurotransmitters are chemical messengers that are released from the axon terminals to cross the synaptic gap and reach the receptor sites of other neurons. In a process known as reuptake, these neurotransmitters attach to the receptor site and are reabsorbed by the neuron to be reused. The steps in the process of synaptic 'message' transmission are:

- The nerve impulse travels down an axon and reaches a synaptic terminal.
- Neurotransmitter(s) is released and fired into the synaptic gap.
- Neurotransmitter(s) binds with receptors on the dendrite of the adjacent neuron.
- Neurotransmitter(s) is taken up by the post-synaptic neuron.
- The 'message' will continue to be passed in this way.

Neurotransmitters play a role in the way we behave, learn, feel and sleep. Some play a role in mental illnesses:

- Dopamine: correlated with movement, attention and learning. Too much dopamine has been associated with schizophrenia.
- Norepinephrine: too little norepinephrine has been associated with depression, while an excess has been associated with schizophrenia.
- Serotonin: plays a role in mood and aggressive behaviour. Too little serotonin is associated with depression and OCD.
- Endorphins: involved in pain relief and feelings of pleasure.

Neuron: receives, processes and transmits information through electrical and chemical signals.

Dendrites: the part of the neuron that receives incoming impulses from an adjacent neuron.

Axon: the part of a nerve cell along which impulses are conducted.

Relay neuron: a nerve cell that passes messages within the CNS.

Neurotransmitter: a chemical messenger in the brain.

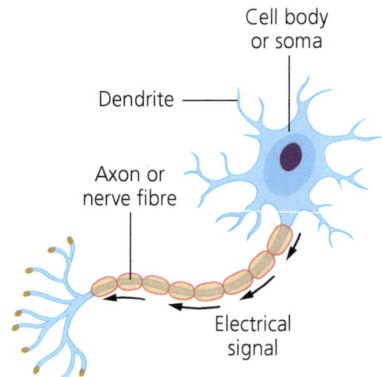

Figure 7.1 A neuron

Revision activity

Write down all the key words relating to synaptic transmission and then use the words to write an outline of how synaptic transmission occurs.

Excitation and inhibition and how these processes interact

Some neurons in the CNS release neurotransmitters that excite other neurons, and some inhibit (prevent) neuronal activity.

Excitatory neurotransmitters are the neurons that conduct the action potential (AP) to release a neurotransmitter and they affect the postsynaptic neurons. What always causes a neuron to release any neurotransmitter (whether it is excitatory or inhibitory) is an action potential. All excitatory neurotransmitters cause sodium ions to flow in and the cell becomes less negative on the inside. These excitatory neurotransmitters create a local increase of permeability of sodium ion channels, which leads to a local depolarisation that is known as an excitatory postsynaptic potential (EPSP) because we are exciting the postsynaptic cell.

Inhibitory neurotransmitters: if an AP goes down the synaptic knob of another neuron and releases an inhibitory neurotransmitter, it is going to be activating different receptor sites on the cell membrane of the postsynaptic cell. When an inhibitory neurotransmitter causes an opening of potassium ion channels, this leads to an inhibitory postsynaptic potential (IPSP) because it is going to be less likely to generate an AP. Whether a neuron generates an AP or not depends on the overall sum of EPSPs and IPSPs occurring in the neuron at any moment in time.

Hebb's theory of learning and neuronal growth

Hebb (1949) was interested in how the function of the brain links to the workings of the mind, especially learning and memory. Hebb stated:

'When an axon of cell A is near enough to excite cell B and repeatedly or persistently takes part in firing it, some growth process or metabolic change takes place in one or both cells such that A's efficiency, as one of the cells firing B, is increased.'

In Hebb's law, this is often paraphrased as 'neurons that fire together wire together'.

Hebb called the combination of neurons which could be grouped together as one processing unit 'cell assemblies'. Hebb's theory influenced how psychologists understood the processing of stimuli within the mind and also opened up the way to develop computers that mimic the working of the human neural pathways, known as artificial neural networks.

Hebb's theory proposed that the more pre- and postsynaptic transmission occurs, the more it will strengthen the connections between the neurons involved and lead to neuronal growth. Hebb suggests that continual firing of an adjacent neuron by the same neuron will eventually form a 'cell assembly' or memory trace. Hebb showed that the biological activity of the brain is related to cognitive functions supporting the area of cognitive neuroscience.

> **Exam tip**
>
> According to Hebb's theory, the more we fire the neurons, the stronger the memory trace – therefore, you need to revise throughout the course and not leave it to the last minute!

Structure and function of the brain

Brain structure

The brain is divided into two symmetrical hemispheres: left (language, the 'rational' half of the brain, associated with analytical thinking and logical abilities) and right (more involved with musical and artistic abilities). The brain is divided into four lobes – frontal lobe, temporal lobe, parietal lobe and occipital lobe – which have different locations and functions that support the responses and actions of the human body.

- **Frontal lobe:** involved in motor skills (including speech) and cognitive functions. The motor centre of the brain, the precentral gyrus, is located in the rear of the frontal lobe, receives connections from the **somatosensory** portion in the parietal lobe, and processes and initiates motor functions.
- **Temporal lobe:** involved in primary auditory perception, such as hearing, and holds the primary auditory cortex. The primary auditory cortex receives sensory information from the ears and secondary areas process the information into meaningful units such as speech and words. Within the temporal lobe, the basal ganglia work with the cerebellum to coordinate fine motions, such as fingertip movements.
- **Parietal lobe:** receives and processes all somatosensory input from the body (touch, pain). Fibres from the spinal cord are distributed by the thalamus to various parts of the parietal lobe. The rear of the parietal lobe has a section called Wernicke's area, which is important for understanding auditory and visual information associated with language.
- **Occipital lobe:** responsible for processing visual information from the eyes. This is where the mind interprets colour, depth cues, shapes and reading. The occipital lobe contains different areas linked to visual communication.
- **Cerebellum:** located at the base of the brain and controls movement through the muscular system. This includes both voluntary movements such as walking or throwing a ball, and **involuntary movements** such as reflexes, for example, if you touch something hot.

Somatosensory: receiving information through touch and the sense of position and movement.

Involuntary movement: movement not under our conscious control, for example reflexes.

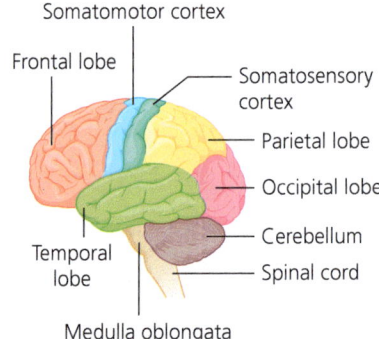

Figure 7.2 **The structure of the human brain**

Localisation of function in the brain: motor, somatosensory, visual, auditory and language areas

Localisation of function in the brain is the theory that specific areas of the brain are associated with particular physical and psychological functions. The following areas of the brain are linked to the specific functions:

- **Motor:** the frontal lobe is involved in motor skills (including speech) and cognitive functions. The motor centre of the brain, the precentral gyrus, is located in the rear of the frontal lobe, receives connections from the somatosensory portion in the parietal lobe, and processes and initiates motor functions.
- **Somatosensory:** this area is located in the parietal lobe and receives incoming sensory information from the skin to produce sensations related to pain and temperature. Different parts of the somatosensory area receive messages from various locations of the body.
- **Visual:** the occipital lobe is responsible for **visual processing**. Information from the right-hand side visual field is processed in the

Localisation of function in the brain: different areas of the brain are responsible for specific functions in the body.

Visual processing: receiving information through the eyes and interpreting the visual information.

left hemisphere, and information from the left-hand side visual field is processed in the right hemisphere.

- **Auditory:** the auditory area is located in the temporal lobe and is responsible for analysing and processing acoustic information (**auditory processing**). The rear of the parietal lobe has a section called Wernicke's area, which is important for understanding auditory information associated with language.
- **Language:** this is restricted to the left side of the brain. Broca (1880s) identified a small area in the left frontal lobe which is responsible for speech production. Damage to Broca's area causes Broca's aphasia which is characterised by speech that is slow and lacking in fluency.

> **Auditory processing**: receiving information through the ears and interpreting the auditory information.

> **Revision activity**
>
> Draw the brain to show the lobes and then label the areas, showing the various functions for each part of the brain.

Key study: Penfield's study of the interpretive cortex

Aim: To investigate the working of the conscious mind to show localised brain functioning.

Method: The participants were patients who were undergoing open brain surgery whilst they were conscious. The procedure was painless as the brain has no sense receptors and the patients required the surgery. Penfield was able to stimulate areas of the brain to demonstrate localised functioning.

Results: When her left temporal lobe was stimulated, one patient reported, 'I had a dream, I had a book under my arm. I was talking to a man. The man was trying to reassure me not to worry about the book.' When they stimulated the temporal cortex, one patient reported hearing a complete orchestration, a voice or a piano. One patient heard the music and saw the man that was playing it at a piano.

Conclusion: Psychological functions are controlled by different areas of the brain supporting the theory of localised functioning of the brain.

Evaluation of Penfield's study

Penfield could access live participants to show the direct effects of stimulating different parts of the brain.

However, the study used the case study method and all of the patients were epileptic, so the findings can't be generalised to people who do not have epilepsy.

> **Revision activity**
>
> Make a cue card to summarise Penfield's study.

> **Exam tip**
>
> Practise summarising the areas of the brain and labelling diagrams. You can then add the labels to explain how the areas work and their function.

Introduction to neuropsychology

REVISED

Cognitive neuroscience: how the structure and function of the brain relate to behaviour and cognition

Cognitive neuroscience is the scientific field that is concerned with the study of the biological processes and aspects of the brain that underlie cognition, with a specific focus on the neural connections in the brain which are involved in a mental process. Cognitive neuroscientists are interested in how brain activity links to cognition, for example how locations of the brain are linked to language, perception and attention. This area of psychology is growing, particularly as we are now able to show brain activity whilst a person completes a cognitive task.

> **Cognitive neuroscience**: the scientific study of the biological processes of the brain that underlie cognition.

Use of scanning techniques to identify brain functioning: CT, PET and fMRI scans

A computed axial tomography (CT) scan uses a series of x-rays of the head taken from many different directions. Typically used for viewing brain injuries, CT scanning uses a computer program that performs a numerical calculation to estimate how much of an x-ray beam is absorbed in a small volume of the brain. The information is presented as a series of cross sections of the brain.

Functional magnetic resonance imaging (fMRI) uses MR imaging to measure the tiny metabolic changes that take place in an active part of the brain. fMRI is used to examine the anatomy of the brain and to determine which part of the brain is handling critical functions such as thought, speech, movement and sensation (brain mapping). fMRI is also used to assess the effects of stroke, trauma or degenerative disease on brain function and to monitor the growth and function of brain tumours. The advantage of using fMRI is that it provides a non-invasive means of finding out which parts of the brain are active and the level of activity.

Positron Emission Tomography (PET) uses small amounts of radioactive material called radiotracers, a special camera and a computer to help evaluate organ and tissue functions. By identifying changes at the cellular level, a PET scan may detect the early onset of disease. A PET scan may be used to locate a part of the brain showing abnormal levels of activity. In most PET scans a radiotracer called fluorodeoxyglucose (FDG) is used, which is similar to naturally occurring glucose (a type of sugar) so the body treats it in a similar way. By analysing the areas where the radiotracer does and doesn't build up, it's possible to work out how well certain body functions are working and identify any abnormalities.

CT scan: A Computed Axial Tomography (CT) scan.

fMRI scan: functional Magnetic Resonance Imaging (fMRI) scan.

PET scan: Positron Emission Tomography (PET) scan.

Revision activity

Bullet point the procedure that is used in each of the brain imaging techniques. Include how they work and what they show.

Key study: Tulving's 'gold' memory study

Aim: To test the link between types of memory (episodic and semantic) and brain activity.

Method: Six participants took part in the case study and were asked to recall a past experience, for example a book they had read (episodic memory) and knowledge they had learned, for example through reading a book (semantic memory). The memories were both recent and from the past. After 60 seconds of beginning to recall, they were injected with a gold isotope into the blood stream to show which brain areas were active during the memory activity. Tulving used a PET scan to measure the hot spots of brain activity.

Results: The results from three of the participants showed that recall from semantic memory produced more activity from the parietal and occipital lobes and cerebral cortex, whereas in episodic memory recall there was more activity in the frontal and temporal lobes.

Conclusion: Overall the results show the distinction between episodic and semantic memories.

Evaluation of Tulving's study

The study was ethical as all participants were willing volunteers and the isotope, although radioactive, was a very mild dose and only active for 30 seconds.

The study used PET scans to measure brain activity which is an objective measure; this makes the study more reliable.

Only half of the participants' results were consistent and could be included which makes the sample very small and not representative of the target population.

The researchers had no way of knowing if the participants followed their instructions and remembered the correct information.

How neurological damage, e.g. stroke or injury, can affect motor abilities and behaviour

Neurological damage to the brain can lead to life-changing consequences. These can include paralysis and stroke.

Any damage to the spinal cord can lead to loss of muscle and the nervous system can no longer work. The severity of loss depends on where the damage is; for example, if the damage is in the neck, then messages can no longer be relayed throughout the body to allow movement and paralysis will be from below the injury site. In the case of a lower back injury, the paralysis will be to the legs and lower back.

A stroke is where there is cell damage to the brain either due to a lack of blood flow or a bleed in the brain. The brain cells rely on oxygen and nutrients from the blood or they will be damaged and the localised functions from the part of the brain will be affected.

Revision activity

Research brain injury in sport. There are some recent articles relating to heading the ball in football and how it can lead to neurological damage.

Summary

You should now be able to demonstrate and apply knowledge and understanding of psychological ideas, processes, procedures and theories, and analyse and evaluate psychological ideas, information, processes and procedures in relation to:

Structure and function of the nervous system:
- The divisions of the human nervous system: central and peripheral (somatic and autonomic)
- The autonomic nervous system
- The fight or flight response
- The James–Lange theory of emotion.

Neuron structure and function:
- Sensory, relay and motor neurons
- Synaptic transmission: release and reuptake of neurotransmitters
- Excitation and inhibition

- Hebb's theory of learning and neuronal growth.

Structure and function of the brain:
- Brain structure: frontal lobe, temporal lobe, parietal lobe, occipital lobe and cerebellum
- Basic function of these structures
- Localisation of function in the brain: motor, somatosensory, visual, auditory and language areas
- Penfield's study of the interpretive cortex.

An introduction to neuropsychology:
- Cognitive neuroscience: how the structure and function of the brain relate to behaviour and cognition
- Scanning techniques to identify brain functioning: CT, PET and fMRI scans
- Tulving's 'gold' memory study
- Neurological damage, e.g. stroke or injury, can affect motor abilities and behaviour.

Now test yourself

TESTED

1 Which function is not controlled by the brain stem?
   A   Heartbeat ☐
   B   Breathing ☐
   C   Decision making ☐
   D   Digestion ☐
2 Fill in the gaps.
   (a) The _____ axis is responsible for arousing the ANS in response to a threat.
   (b) The _____ of the nervous system stimulates the adrenal gland to release adrenaline, noradrenaline and corticosteroids into the bloodstream.
   (c) The increase in _____ produces the physiological reactions, such as increased heart rate and blood pressure.
   (d) After the threat is gone, it takes _____ for the body to return to its pre-arousal levels.

→

3 Fill in the gaps.
  (a) The _____ theory of emotion suggests that emotions are a result of physiological responses, and not their cause.
  (b) The perception of _____ stimuli is followed by specific physiological reactions such as release of adrenaline and flight reaction.
  (c) The brain interprets the specific physiological changes as the _____ .
  (d) 'I'm _____ because my heart is racing and I am _____ .'
4 Which of the following is not one of the four lobes of the brain?
  A   Frontal ☐
  B   Prefrontal cortex ☐
  C   Occipital ☐
  D   Parietal ☐
5 Draw a neuron and describe the function of motor, sensory and relay neurons.
6 Fill in the gaps.
  (a) _____ travels down an axon and reaches a synaptic terminal.
  (b) This triggers the release of _____ and these are fired into the synaptic gap.
  (c) The neurotransmitter binds with receptors on the _____ of the adjacent neuron.
  (d) If successfully transmitted, the neurotransmitter is taken up by the _____ neuron. The message will continue to be passed in this way via _____ .
7 Outline Hebb's theory of learning and neuronal growth.

Answers on pp.105–6

Exam practice

1 Which lobe is responsible for processing visual information from the eyes? This is where the mind interprets colour, depth cues, and shapes. Shade one box only. [1 mark]
  A   The parietal lobe ☐
  B   The occipital lobe ☐
  C   The frontal lobe ☐
  D   The temporal lobe ☐
2 Evaluate Penfield's study of the interpretive cortex. [4 marks]
3 Outline the function of a sensory neuron. [2 marks]
4 Christian and Jenna are watching a horror film about vampires. The screen is blank when suddenly a vampire jumps out and Jenna screams and Christian jumps up from his seat.
  (a) From your knowledge of the fight or flight response, briefly explain what is happening to Jenna and Christian. [4 marks]
  (b) Outline the James–Lange theory of emotion. [4 marks]
  (c) Identify and explain **one** criticism of the James–Lange theory of emotion. [4 marks]
5 Dopamine is a neurotransmitter associated with movement, attention and learning.
  Too much dopamine has been associated with schizophrenia.
  (a) Outline synaptic transmission. [4 marks]
  (b) Describe the difference between excitatory and inhibitory neurotransmitters. [5 marks]

Answers on p.112

> **Exam tip**
>
> Watch out for questions like this. You need to refer to the scenario in your answer.

4 Psychological problems

Key concepts

Characteristics of mental health

Cultural variations in beliefs about mental health problems

Increased challenges of modern living

Increased recognition of the nature of mental health problems and lessening of social stigma

Individual effects, e.g. damage to relationships, difficulties coping with day-to-day life, negative impact on physical wellbeing

Social effects, e.g. need for more social care, increased crime rates, implications for the economy

Differences between unipolar depression, bipolar depression and sadness

Use of International Classification of Diseases in diagnosing unipolar depression

Interventions or therapies for depression

Biological explanation (influence of nature): imbalance of neurotransmitters

Psychological explanation (influence of nurture): negative schemas and attributions

Use of antidepressant medications

Cognitive behaviour therapy (CBT)

How therapies and interventions improve mental health; reductionist and holistic perspectives on therapies for depression

Wiles' study of the effectiveness of CBT

The difference between addiction/dependence and substance misuse/abuse

Use of International Classification of Diseases in diagnosing addiction (dependence syndrome)

Interventions or therapies for addiction

Biological explanation (influence of nature): hereditary factors/genetic vulnerability

Kaij's twin study of alcohol abuse

Psychological explanation (influence of nurture): peer influence

Aversion therapy

Self-management programmes, e.g. self-help groups, 12 step recovery programmes

How therapies and interventions improve mental health; reductionist and holistic perspectives on therapies for addiction

An introduction to mental health

REVISED

Mental health is an important aspect of life and in our present-day lives has become a focus of discussion and concern. The need for positive mental health is a concern for individual and for society and includes social, emotional and psychological **wellbeing** to cope with the demands of life.

Characteristics of mental health

Characteristics of mental health include:
- Positive engagement with society
- Effective **coping** with challenges
- Having satisfying personal relationships
- Being able to make decisions for oneself
- Having a sense of **self-worth**.

Cultural variations in beliefs about mental health problems

Attitudes to mental health problems vary across cultures and can lead to **stigma** and individuals not seeking help when needed.

One of the main problems is the view that mental health problems are a sign of individual weakness and in some cultures, there is stigma attached to the problem.

Although it could be argued that there is still stigma seen in UK culture, the view of mental health problems is changing and moving more in line with physical health problems.

> **Wellbeing**: overall physical, social and psychological health.
>
> **Coping**: the ability to meet the demands of everyday activities.
>
> **Self-worth**: the value we place on ourselves.
>
> **Stigma**: a strong feeling of disapproval towards a behaviour from others.

How the incidence of significant mental health problems changes over time

REVISED

Increased challenges of modern living

One reason behind the rise in mental health problems could be the increased challenges of modern life. One challenge is the use of social media which has been found to be linked to mental health problems in young people; it can lead to problems of social comparison with others as well as social isolation.

A study in the USA found that heavy users of social media were three times more likely to develop depression than those who used social media less regularly. *The Guardian* reported results of a survey of almost 1,500 14 to 24 year olds, which found Instagram increased levels of inadequacy and anxiety.

> **Revision activity**
>
> Read the article in *The Guardian*: 'Facebook and Twitter "harm young people's mental health"': www.theguardian.com/society/2017/may/19/popular-social-media-sites-harm-young-peoples-mental-health

Increased recognition of the nature of mental health problems and lessening of social stigma

According to the charity YoungMinds, one in ten young adults has a diagnosable mental health problem. This could be due to the recognition of the nature of mental health problems across the media and the number of people seeking help for their mental health.

This could also be due to the lessening of social stigma associated with mental health issues which will lead to more open discussion in schools and in family groups and better support for the individual. Overall, we could argue that increased recognition and lessening of the stigma could explain the rise in mental health problems.

Effects of significant mental health problems on individuals and society

Individual effects

Significant mental health problems can be **damaging to relationships** because living with a family member who has a mental health problem can be very stressful. There is the continuous concern for their wellbeing and their future by family and this can lead to family members becoming stressed and anxious as well. According to a Swedish study, one half of family members claimed they had developed psychological or social problems (such as sleeping problems and depression) of their own to such an extent that they also needed help and support.

Mental health problems can result in **difficulties coping with day-to-day life** that others take for granted. This may include motivation to take part in activities that to most people bring enjoyment, such as going out for a meal with friends; this could be problematic for people with social anxiety, eating disorders or depression. They may not be well enough to attend school, college or work.

The effects of mental health problems can additionally lead to a **negative impact on physical wellbeing**. Poor emotional health can weaken the body's immune system. This makes you more likely to get colds and other infections when you are continually anxious. Disorders, such as depression, may lead to problems with sleeping, not looking after oneself and not taking exercise, which can lead to health problems. Eating disorders can lead to extreme weight loss and damage to the heart.

Social effects

One social effect of significant mental health problems includes **the increased need for more social care**. The NHS conducted a report across the hospitals in England, with 80 per cent of the trust managers reporting a significant shortfall in money for mental health services leading to long waiting lists for treatment. The report concludes that children, older people and people in a mental health crisis too often receive inadequate care for conditions such as anxiety, depression and eating disorders.

One possible social effect could be **increased crime rates** linked to mental health disorders. For most mental health problems, there is no increased risk of crime; it is also likely that people with mental health problems are more likely to be the victims of crime. It has been suggested that there is a link between violence and bi-polar disorder due to drug use. There is research from prison populations to show that 49 per cent of female and 29 per cent of male offenders in prisons have mental health problems, though it is not clear if mental health causes the crime or being in prison causes the mental health problem.

Mental health problems have **implications for the economy** due to the cost to the NHS and other agencies who support people with mental health problems. There is a further effect on the economy because the individual may be unable to work due to their mental health problems and then are not able to pay tax and national insurance contributions.

> **Revision activity**
>
> Make a mind map for all the effects of significant mental health problems on individuals and society. Use a different colour for each effect.

> **Exam tip**
>
> In the exam, you need to make sure you are clear about the difference between the effects of mental illness on the individual and the effects on society. You need to be specific in your examples as to why the effects will occur.

Characteristics of clinical depression

Depression is a **mood** disorder associated with varying degrees of sadness; an individual may experience feelings of hopelessness and extreme pessimism about themselves, the world and their future. It is the most common mental health problem with 25 per cent of the UK population likely to have an episode in their lifetime.

Differences between unipolar depression, bipolar depression and sadness

Table 8.1 Differences between unipolar depression, bipolar depression and sadness

Unipolar depression	Bipolar depression	Sadness
Low mood and extreme sadness when there is no reason for feeling low	Periods of low mood followed by episodes of extremely elevated mood and **mania**	Low mood when there is a reason for the mood state, such as grief

International Classification of Diseases in diagnosing unipolar depression

Symptoms include
- Low mood
- Reduced energy levels
- Changes in sleep patterns
- Change in appetite levels
- Decrease in self-confidence.

The diagnosis will be made if symptoms persist for a two-week period and the severity of the illness is based on the number of symptoms the patient is experiencing. The more symptoms, the higher the severity is judged.

Theories of depression

Biological explanation (influence of nature)

Biological explanations for depression argue that the cause is linked to **nature** and genetically determined. From this perspective depression is purely biological and part of our DNA.

Imbalance of neurotransmitters

Depression is linked to an imbalance in the neurotransmitter **serotonin**, which is the chemical messenger in the brain responsible for the firing of neurons and enabling normal brain functioning. Serotonin is linked to sleep, appetite and mood, and patients with depression have low levels of serotonin, as they respond to anti-depressants which increase the levels of serotonin. In post-mortem studies, McNeal and Cimbolic (1986) found lower levels of serotonin by-products in the cerebrospinal fluid of previously suicidal patients, suggesting lower levels of serotonin in the brain. This shows that there is a link between serotonin and depression.

Mood: a temporary state of mind, how we are feeling.

Mania: a heightened state of excitement and hyperactivity.

Symptoms: features that can be used to make a diagnosis.

Revision activity

Write a glossary of the key words and key features of unipolar depression.

Nature: behaviour is influenced by inherited characteristics.

Serotonin: a neurotransmitter linked to mood and regulation of aggression.

Serotonin-based drugs do not always help people who suffer from depression.

Even if drugs that raise serotonin levels reduce depression, this does not mean that low levels of serotonin cause depression. It may be that depression causes the low levels of serotonin.

Psychological explanation (influence of nurture)

Psychological explanations include the influence of **nurture**, which is the extent to which the environment influences our behaviour, including the influence it can have on mental illnesses such as depression.

Nurture: behaviour is influenced by the environment and upbringing.

Schemas: stored information about past experiences that we use to interpret/plan.

Negative schemas

Beck (1967) suggested that depressed individuals have acquired negative **schemas** during childhood and these negative schemas are activated to generate cognitive biases in thought processes to maintain a negative triad, described as a pessimistic view of the self, the world and the future.

Schemas are how we interpret situations and make sense of the world, and early schemas can be affected by rejection or a traumatic event from childhood, such as parental divorce. This leads individuals to a negative schema about themselves as worthless and they continue to see themselves in this way.

Attribution

Gilbert (1984) suggested depression will occur if:
- the individual is aware of uncontrollable factors in their environment
- the individual views the situation as unchangeable
- they blame themselves for their helplessness – internal attribution
- they attribute bad outcomes to personal, stable and global character faults.

Attribution theory is how we perceive events in our lives, such as if we mislay our bag; we might think that we left our bag on the bus (internal attribution) or that someone has deliberately taken our bag (external attribution). A person with depression is more likely to make external attributions, believe life is conspiring against them, and that they have no control over what happens to them, for example, 'Bad things always happen to me.' This leads to a feeling that they have no way of changing life's outcomes and therefore making an effort is a waste of time.

Interventions or therapies for depression

Use of antidepressant medications

The most common antidepressants used for depression are selective serotonin reuptake inhibitors (SSRIs) such as fluoxetine that block the reuptake of serotonin from the synaptic gap, causing levels of the neurotransmitter to increase. These relieve the symptoms of low mood, sleep disturbance and low energy levels.

Martin *et al.* (2001) used scanning techniques to compare the effect of drug therapy and interpersonal therapy on brain function and found similar changes in levels of serotonin in patients who experienced an effect of either treatment. This suggests that life experience does change the biochemistry of the brain.

Cognitive behaviour therapy (CBT)

Cognitive therapies all work in a similar way by first getting the patient to recognise their irrational perceptions, then agreeing on a more realistic approach, and finally putting this into practice in a real-life situation.

Cognitive behaviour therapy (CBT) recognises the importance of changing both behaviour and thinking.

The assumptions underlying CBT are:
● It is our interpretation of events rather than the events themselves that is important.
● Thoughts, behaviours and feelings all influence each other.
● The role of the therapist is to help the patient identify their irrational thoughts and to change their interpretations to get rid of negative biases.
● The patient must change both the way they think and their behaviour.

Butler *et al.* (2006) studied the results from more than 10,000 patients and found that CBT was effective in treating depression (and more successfully than anti-depressants), anxiety disorder, panic disorder and social phobia.

> **Revision activity**
>
> List two differences between biological and psychological therapies.

How interventions and therapies improve mental health

When using treatments to improve mental health, it is important that they are effective in treating the symptoms of the disorder in order to improve overall wellbeing and quality of life. Treatments can follow two main perspectives that are **reductionist** and **holistic**.

Reductionism is reducing the explanation of complex phenomena to one factor such as a biological reason. In the case of mental health, treatments that focus on one neurotransmitter, such as serotonin, can be described as reductionist treatments.

Sometimes reductionist drug treatment can be seen as advantageous as we are able to measure and control the dosage of the selective serotonin reuptake inhibitors. However, it could be argued that reductionist drug treatments alone are not effective because they ignore cognitive and social factors.

The holistic viewpoint takes a broader view of improving mental health and considers a range of options, including drug therapies and CBT.

From a holistic perspective, there may be a number of 'reasons' for a disorder including biological, psychological and social factors. Therefore, treatment should consider all aspects of the individual's life, including improving social factors, for example through family therapy.

Key study: Wiles' study of the effectiveness of CBT

Aim: To test the effectiveness of CBT in patients with drug treatment resistant depression.

Method: Participants were allocated to two groups: 234 received CBT alongside their normal treatment (drug and medical routines), 235 received their normal treatment.

CBT was carried out by a trained therapist and the participants had 12 one-hour sessions.

Results: Over the course of 46 months, 43 per cent of those who had received CBT had improved, reporting at least a 50 per cent reduction in symptoms of depression, compared with 27 per cent who continued with their usual care alone.

Conclusions: CBT is an effective treatment that can be used alongside drug treatments for patients with depression.

Evaluation of Wiles' study

The study is longitudinal, and researchers were able to follow patients over a 12-month period.

The study controls for individual differences as it is following the progress of the same participants throughout the study, which makes the results comparable.

However, not all the participants attended all the sessions. This weakens the argument that CBT is an effective treatment.

Exam tip

Remember that reductionism should not be seen as just a weakness but can be seen as a strength as well. Be prepared to debate the two sides of the argument.

Characteristics of addiction

REVISED

The difference between addiction and dependence

- **Addiction** is a repetitive habit pattern that increases the risk of disease and/or associated personal and social problems. Addictive behaviours are often experienced subjectively as a 'loss of control' – the behaviour continues to occur despite volitional attempts to abstain or moderate use. These habit patterns are typically characterised by immediate gratification (short-term reward), often coupled with delayed harmful effects (long-term costs). **DSM-5** includes 'substance use disorder' for drug addictions, including nicotine, and 'addictive disorders' for non-substance abuse. There is now a separate category for 'gambling disorder'.
- **Dependence** can be physical in nature and is usually experienced with addiction to substances, such as nicotine. Attempts to give up will lead to physical symptoms. It is possible to experience addiction without physical symptoms, for example from non-substance addiction to gambling or addiction to the internet. Additionally, individuals can experience both physical and psychological dependence, for example the attitude and belief that they have about their smoking behaviour, such as 'smoking can reduce my stress levels'.

Addiction: a repetitive habit pattern towards an action or substance such as smoking or gambling.

DSM-5: a diagnostic manual used by health professionals to diagnose mental illness.

Dependence: relying on a substance to control mood or negative consequences of stopping.

The difference between substance misuse/abuse

Many substances produce psychoactive effects that are experienced as pleasure and then will lead to their continued consumption. These can include tea, coffee and other caffeinated drinks and foods high in sugar. Additionally, there are recreational drugs that have short-lived physiological effects. These drugs come in two categories: those that are legal such as alcohol and nicotine, and those that are illegal such as cocaine and heroin.

- **Misuse** of substances is consumption above the normal level that would be expected in a typical lifestyle; for example, consuming more than the recommended levels of alcohol and binge drinking.
- **Abuse** occurs when the level of misuse becomes dangerous and can lead to serious addiction for which a diagnosis of dependence syndrome would be made.

Use of International Classification of Diseases in diagnosing addiction (dependence syndrome)

The tenth revision of the International Classification of Diseases (ICD-10) defines dependence syndrome as being a cluster of physiological, behavioural and cognitive phenomena in which the use of a substance, or a class of substances, takes on a much higher priority for an individual than other behaviours that once had greater value.

The term 'dependence' has replaced the term 'addiction' and symptoms can include:

- A strong desire, or sense of compulsion, to take the substance
- Difficulties in controlling substance-taking behaviour in terms of its onset, termination or levels of use
- A physiological withdrawal state when substance use has ceased or has been reduced, as evidenced by: the characteristic withdrawal syndrome for the substance; or use of the same (or closely related) substance with the intention of relieving or avoiding withdrawal symptoms
- Progressive neglect of alternative pleasures or interests because of psychoactive substance use, increased amount of time necessary to obtain or take the substance or to recover from its effects.

Theories of addiction

REVISED

Biological explanation (influence of nature): hereditary factors/genetic vulnerability

The genetic model suggests that there is a genetic disposition towards addictive behaviour and that an addictive personality may be genetically determined. Research in this area analyses the genetic structure of the individual and their role in the prevalence of addictive behaviours.

Twins can be either monozygotic (identical), meaning that they develop from one zygote, which splits and forms two embryos, or dizygotic (fraternal), meaning that the twins develop from two different eggs and each egg is fertilised by its own sperm cell. Research has focused on twin studies to show the genetic link between identical (MZ) and non-identical (DZ) twins. As MZ twins share exactly the same genetic makeup and DZ twins share only 50 per cent, it allows psychologists to make useful comparisons measured using concordance rate as percentages. For example, is there a greater risk of becoming a smoker if your parents smoke?

Hughes (1986) compared two groups of adolescents. One group lived with family members who smoked, and the other group lived with family members who did not smoke. Findings showed that 52 per cent of those who lived with smokers smoked compared to 20 per cent of those living with non-smokers.

Hall *et al.* (2002) reported on a recent adoption study which found a strong association between adoptees and their biological siblings smoking and between male adoptees and their biological mother.

Key study: Kaij's twin study of alcohol abuse

Aim: To test whether alcohol abuse is a hereditary factor.

Method: The study was carried out in Sweden with 174 pairs of twins born since 1880, including 48 pairs of monozygotic twins and 126 pairs of dizygotic twins. All the pairs of twins were male and were identified from public registers of people with alcoholism. Participants were interviewed by the researchers and asked to complete questionnaires. From the results of the interviews and the questionnaires, the participants were categorised in five groups according to the level of alcoholism.

Results: 58 per cent of the MZ twins were in the same category for alcohol compared to 28 per cent of the DZ twins.

Conclusion: There are hereditary factors involved with alcohol use and abuse.

Evaluation of Kaij's study

Kaij managed to gather a large sample to take part in the research, which makes the results more generalisable.

All the participants were male and not representative of females with alcoholism.

The rates of twins in the same category is not conclusive as it should be 100 per cent for MZ twins and 50 per cent for DZ twins if purely based on genetics.

Revision activity

Make a table for addiction, dependence, misuse and abuse and write the definition for each to use as revision.

Psychological explanation (influence of nurture): peer influence

Family attitudes towards recreational drugs, such as nicotine, can also influence adolescent behaviour; for example, if parents have a positive attitude to smoking, this can be a risk factor for adolescent smoking.

Family and peers provide role models which shape behaviour, particularly if reinforced as suggested by social learning theory. Peer pressure has been linked to first time use of nicotine and recreational drugs, but peer pressure is more prevalent in teenage years and decreases with age. McAlister (1984) found that increased levels of smoking were linked to peer pressure and encouragement.

Evaluation of explanations for addiction

One problem with genetic explanations for addictive behaviour is that they are focused on the nature side of the nature/nurture debate and ignore environmental influences on addictive behaviour.

Alternatively, family and peers only suggest nurture or environmental risks.

A better explanation could consider the influence of both nature and nurture, for example the diathesis stress model.

Another weakness is that research suggests a link between several factors and addictive behaviour. This means there is no cause and effect established and we cannot say that peers or genetics cause addiction.

Identifying risk factors such as the influence of family and peers has application as they can lead to educational campaigns to help reduce the initiation of substance abuse in vulnerable teenagers.

Interventions or therapies for addiction

Addiction is a problem for the individual and may cause them to feel distress. It is therefore important to help individuals to cease the behaviour that is addictive.

Aversion therapy

Aversion therapy is based on the behavioural approach that addiction is caused by classical conditioning. Aversion therapy is the pairing of an aversive stimulus with a specific addiction response; this, therefore, pairs the stimulus with an unpleasant response rather than a pleasant one. For example, alcoholics may be prescribed an emetic so that if they drink alcohol, they will vomit. This will lead to alcohol being associated with vomiting rather than pleasure, discouraging alcoholics from drinking.

Covert sensitisation is a milder form of aversion therapy where the addict will use imagery to create a negative association with the behaviour. For example, a sugar addict may use imagery to visualise a slice of chocolate cake and then visualise it covered in mud. They will then associate the cake with an unpleasant experience rather than a pleasant one.

Evaluation of aversion therapy

Aversion therapy is based on the behavioural approach and it ignores any physiological changes that occur due to use of a substance, such as alcohol increasing the dopamine in the brain pleasure pathway.

The use of imagery in covert sensitisation would be seen as a more ethical way to treat the addiction rather than full aversion therapy.

Self-management programmes

Many individuals wish to cease an addictive behaviour such as smoking or drinking alcohol. Many follow programmes that are available through **self-help groups** including Alcoholics Anonymous and groups for quitting smoking. These work on the basis that social support can help with addictions, particularly as all the members of the group are going through the same process or may be further along in the process and able to provide motivation. There is usually a requirement to attend group meetings, and to admit one has a problem with addictive behaviour.

Many support groups available to help people self-manage their progress follow the **12-step recovery programme**, including Alcoholics Anonymous and Narcotics Anonymous. The original programme is strongly rooted in spirituality although many non-religious participants have found benefit from the programme. The steps progress from 'we admit we have no control over the alcohol and that our lives have become unmanageable', to 'we have had a spiritual awakening as the result of these steps'.

Evaluation of self-management programmes

This self-managed programme treatment ignores any physiological changes that occur due to use of a substance, such as alcohol increasing the dopamine in the brain pleasure pathway.

The success of self-managed treatment relies on high levels of motivation from the individual. This requires very high levels of willpower and self-efficacy to complete.

Revision activity

Imagine you are going to set up an addiction awareness programme in your school. How could you use the role of peers to reduce addiction?

Exam tip

If you include theories in your answer that can be applied to other behaviours, for example social learning theory, make sure it is clear that you are linking your explanation to addiction.

Summary

You should now be able to demonstrate and apply knowledge and understanding of psychological ideas, processes, procedures and theories, and analyse and evaluate psychological ideas, information, processes and procedures in relation to:

An introduction to mental health:
- Characteristics of mental health, e.g. positive engagement with society, effective coping with challenges
- Cultural variations in beliefs about mental health problems.

How the incidence of significant mental health problems changes over time:
- Increased challenges of modern living, e.g. isolation
- Increased recognition of the nature of mental health problems and lessening of social stigma.

Effects of significant mental health problems on individuals and society:
- Individual effects, e.g. damage to relationships, difficulties coping with day-to-day life, negative impact on physical wellbeing
- Social effects, e.g. need for more social care, increased crime rates, implications for the economy.

Characteristics of clinical depression:
- Differences between unipolar depression, bipolar depression and sadness
- The use of International Classification of Diseases in diagnosing unipolar depression: number and severity of symptoms including low mood, reduced energy levels, changes in sleep patterns and appetite levels, decrease in self-confidence.

Theories of depression:
- Biological explanation (influence of nature): imbalance of neurotransmitters, e.g. serotonin in the brain
- Psychological explanation (influence of nurture): negative schemas and attributions.

Interventions or therapies for depression:
- Use of antidepressant medications
- Cognitive behaviour therapy (CBT)
- How these improve mental health; reductionist and holistic perspectives. Wiles' study of the effectiveness of CBT.

Characteristics of addiction:
- The difference between addiction/dependence and substance misuse/abuse
- The use of International Classification of Diseases in diagnosing addiction (dependence syndrome), including a strong desire to use substance(s) despite harmful consequences, difficulty in controlling use, a higher priority given to the substance(s) than to other activities or obligations.

Theories of addiction:
- Biological explanation (influence of nature): hereditary factors/genetic vulnerability. Kaij's twin study of alcohol abuse
- Psychological explanation (influence of nurture): peer influence.

Interventions or therapies for addiction:
- Aversion therapy
- Self-management programmes, e.g. self-help groups, 12-step recovery programmes
- How these improve mental health; reductionist and holistic perspectives.

Now test yourself

1 Which of the following is **not** a sign of mental health?
   A   Positive engagement with society ☐
   B   Effective coping with challenges ☐
   C   Lacking self-worth ☐
   D   Able to make decisions for oneself ☐
2 Which of the following is not a symptom of unipolar depression?
   A   Increased aggression ☐
   B   Changed sleep patterns ☐
   C   Changed appetite levels ☐
   D   Decreased self-confidence. ☐
3 Explain how stigma towards mental health has changed in recent times.
4 Fill in the gaps.
   (a)   Unipolar depression includes symptoms such as _____ and _____ .
   (b)   The diagnosis will be made if symptoms persist for a _____ period.
   (c)   The _____ of the illness is based on the _____ of symptoms the patient is experiencing.
   (d)   The more symptoms, the _____ the severity is judged.
5 Describe the effects of significant mental health problems on individuals and society.
6 Outline the role of serotonin in unipolar depression.
7 **Outline and evaluate** the use of CBT to treat unipolar depression.
8 Evaluate the reductionist view of improving mental health.

Answers on p.106

Exam practice

1 Which of the following is **not** a symptom of unipolar depression? Shade one box only. [1 mark]
   A   Low mood ☐
   B   Problems with sleeping ☐
   C   Change in appetite ☐
   D   Hallucinations ☐
2 Which of the following is **not** a symptom of dependence syndrome? [1 mark]
   A   A strong desire, or sense of compulsion, to take the substance ☐
   B   Difficulties in controlling substance-taking behaviour in terms of levels of use ☐
   C   Active avoidance of the substance to reduce the behaviour ☐
   D   Progressive neglect of alternative pleasures or interests because of psychoactive substance use ☐
3 Describe one study on the effectiveness of CBT as a treatment for depression and evaluate the methods used. [8 marks]
4 Discuss the view that unipolar depression is influenced by nature. [6 marks]
5 The most common antidepressants used for treating depression are selective serotonin reuptake inhibitors (SSRIs) such as fluoxetine. Outline the use of drugs to treat depression. [4 marks]
6 Describe the difference between addiction and dependence. [5 marks]
7 Discuss the view that addiction is influenced by nature. [6 marks]
8 Outline self-management programmes for the treatment of addiction. [4 marks]

Answers on pp.112–13

Now test yourself answers

Paper 1: Cognition and behaviour

1 Memory

1 **(a)** B 7 plus or minus 2 chunks

   (b) D about 30 seconds

   (c) C episodic memory

   (d) B acoustically

2 **(a)** The capacity of memory in STM is approximately 'seven plus or minus two' pieces of information.

   (b) STM has limited capacity, approximately seven to nine pieces of information, but LTM has unlimited capacity. Information in STM has limited duration, about 30 seconds, but information in LTM may last a lifetime.

   (c) The primacy effect is when the first items from a list of information are recalled better and the recency effect is when the last items of information from a list are recalled better.

   (d) The primacy effect happens because the first items of information have been transferred to LTM, and the recency effect happens because the last items of information are still in STM and this supports the theory of two separate memory stores in the multi-store model.

   (e) Episodic memory is the collection of your past personal experiences (autobiographical events) that occurred at particular times and in particular places; for example, remembering your 16th birthday is an episodic memory.

   (f) Procedural memory stores information on how to perform certain procedures, such as walking, talking, typing, playing the piano, riding a bike. Procedural memories do not involve conscious thought.

   (g) Semantic memory allows us to give meaning to words and sentences and to understand language.

3 **(a)** 'Retrieval failure' means that a memory cannot be retrieved.

   (b) According to the multi-store model of memory, the capacity of STM is between five and nine items of information. As the list of words was read to them, they had no time to rehearse the information, so information in STM would be displaced by subsequent information.

   (c) When we store a new memory, we also store information about the situation and when we come to the same situation again, these retrieval cues can trigger the memory of the situation.

   (d) External retrieval cues are in the environment, for example the smell of the place where the memory was formed, but internal retrieval cues are the state inside the person such as the mood we were in when the memory was formed.

   (e) The students who were tested in the same room where they learned the bird words would have had the same external retrieval cues to help them remember the words, but the students who were tested in a different room would have had no matching retrieval cues to help them remember the bird words.

4 **(a)** The aim of the study was to see if suggestion could create a false memory.

   (b) There were 24 participants, three males and 21 females, ranging in age from 18 to 53, and for each participant a relative was also contacted.

   (c) One criticism is that ethical issues arise when participants are deceived and are left with the implanted false memory about their childhood. Even though at the end of the study the participants were told that the Lost in the Mall story was not true, participants may still have the false memory.

   (d) **Duration of event:** the longer we watch, the more likely we are to remember details. **Violence distraction:** people have a better memory for non-violent events. **Amount of time between an event and recall:** the longer the time, the worse the recall. **Anxiety:** highly emotional events may be either more memorable or less memorable than everyday events.

2 Perception

1 **(a)** Motion parallax is a **monocular** depth cue in which we view objects that are closer to us as moving faster than objects that are further away from us.

   (b) We judge **depth** in the real world in three dimensions.

(c) Monocular depth cues are clues to **distance** that only need one eye.

(d) Objects making bigger images on the retina are perceived as being **nearer** than objects making smaller images.

(e) Linear perspective is a **depth cue** because lines which are parallel appear to converge.

(f) Binocular depth cues provide depth information when viewing a scene with **both** eyes.

(g) **Retinal disparity** is the information derived from the different projection of objects onto the retina of each eye to judge depth.

(h) Sensation is the **physical** process of receiving information from the environment through the senses such as hearing, taste, smell and vision.

(i) Perception is the **cognitive** process by which we transform sensory data into meaningful sounds and images.

2 **Sensation** is a physical process of receiving information from the environment through the senses such as hearing and vision, but **perception** is the cognitive process by which we transform sensory data into sounds and images.

3 One type of visual constancy is our ability to perceive that an object remains the same even when viewed from a different angle so that the object projects different images onto the retinas in our eyes. Different types of visual constancy are shape, colour, size, brightness and location.

4 Linear perspective is used by artists as a depth cue; parallel lines in the real world never meet, but lines such as railway lines are drawn appearing to get narrower (to converge) in the distance.

5

The Müller-Lyer illusion

6 One explanation is that because we live in a 'carpentered world' the brain is used to interpreting angles as far and near corners, so when looking at the Müller-Lyer arrows, the line with outward pointing arrows is perceived as longer.

7 Gibson's theory suggests that perception is **innate and that no learning is required**. Gibson's theory is nature not nurture, and for Gibson the information we receive about objects allows us to interact directly with the environment. Gibson theorised that the pattern of light reaching the eye provides unambiguous information about the layout of objects in space. For example, if the flow of optical information appears to be coming from a point, it means you are moving towards it. If the optic array is moving towards the point, you are moving away from it.

3 Development

1 **B** The cerebral cortex

2 **A** Dendrites receive incoming signals and axons relay outgoing signals to other neurons.

3 **A** At the age of three, the brain has up to twice as many synapses as it has at the age of 20.

4 **B** Four

5 **A** Egocentric

6 (a) A schema is a **mental** structure and as we age we develop schemas for abstract concepts.

(b) Piaget proposed that if new experience does not match existing schemas a state of **disequilibrium** is produced.

(c) **Assimilation** occurs when new information can be fitted into the child's current understanding of the world.

(d) The ability to **conserve** has been developed when a child understands that quantity does not change when appearance changes.

7 **B** Sensorimotor, pre-operational, concrete operational, formal operations

8 **B** The inability to understand that people still exist when out of sight

9 **D** Unable to perform mental transformations without a real object to manipulate

10 **C** Mess up the rows of counters

11 **A** Fixed and growth mindset

12 **D** The content's best modality

4 Research methods

1 **B** A prediction that the IV will have no effect

2 **B** An independent variable

3 **C** The participants do not know they are being observed

4 **D** Low levels of validity because participants may not give true answers

5 (a) A null hypothesis

(b) A field experiment is a way of conducting research in an everyday environment and one difference is that in a field experiment there is an increase in the naturalness of the setting and a decrease in the level of control that the experimenter is able to achieve.

(c) High levels of control in experimental methods allow extraneous variables that might affect the IV or the DV to be minimised. The researcher can be sure that any changes in the DV are the result of changes in the IV.

(d) Experimental settings may not measure how people behave outside in their everyday lives.

(e) No explanation for the observed behaviour is gained because the observer counts instances of behaviour but does not ask participants to explain why they acted as they did.

(f) Questionnaires can be used with large samples of participants and can be used again with a different sample to allow research to be replicated to test reliability.

(g) When using questionnaires, we cannot assume that participants will tell the truth, and bias, such as social desirability bias, may lead to invalid results.

(h) The independent variable (IV) is the variable we manipulate in experimental research.

(i) The dependent variable (DV) is the variable we measure in experimental research.

(j) Behaviour can be observed in its usual setting.

(k) In an overt observation, participants know they are being observed and this reduces validity due to participants changing their behaviour and increased demand characteristics.

(l) A case study gives a detailed picture of the life and experiences of one individual, but one person cannot be a representative sample of the wider population, so the findings cannot be applied to explain the behaviour of anyone else.

(m) This was not a random sample as in a random sample everyone in the whole population of interest has an equal chance of being selected.

6 (a) One ethical issue to be considered would be **consent of the participants**. The investigator should inform the participants of all aspects of the research that might reasonably be expected to influence willingness to participate. Also, where research involves people under the age of 16, consent should be obtained from parents or from those *in loco parentis*. Another issue would be **confidentiality:** participants in psychological research have a right to expect that information they provide will be treated confidentially and, if published, will not be identifiable as theirs.

(b) Alternative hypothesis

7 (a) A random sample involves having the names of the target population and giving everyone an equal chance of being selected, so the names of the 53 psychology students could be written on slips of paper and put in a box and then 20 slips selected who would be the random sample.

(b) Opportunity samples are almost always biased samples, as who participates is dependent on who is asked and who happens to be available locally at the time.

(c) To achieve a systematic sample of 20 participants you would select every 10th name from the list of 200 names and stop when you have selected 10 names.

(d) In an experiment having an independent design, different participants are used in each of the conditions, but in an experiment having a repeated measures design, the same participants are used in each of the conditions.

(e) Suggested answers: giving to charity collectors; holding shop doors open for others; stepping out of the way to allow others to pass; giving money to homeless people on the street; buying a copy of *Big Issue*.

8 **A** 5×10^3

9 a) **D** 4 : 1

b) In total there are 20 birds, 16 are ducks so $\frac{16}{20}$ x 100, thus 80%

c) In total there are 20 birds, 4 are swans, so $\frac{4}{20}$ x 100 = 20%

d) $\frac{4}{20}$, corrected to $\frac{2}{10}$, corrected to $\frac{1}{5}$ of the birds flew away.

10 $\frac{3}{4}$ of the audience was male.

11 35 – 20 = 15, so the ratio was 20 chocolate cakes to 15 other flavours. Thus, the ratio was 4 : 3; there were 4 chocolate cakes to every 3 other flavours.

12

(a) $\frac{2}{100}$ = 2%

(b) $\frac{1}{10}$ = 1%

(c) $\frac{5}{20}$ = 25%

(d) $\frac{20}{100}$ = 20%

13 **A** (£3.99 rounded up to £4) + (£4.99 rounded up to £5) + (£2.85 rounded up to £3.00) = £12

14 585.48 rounded up = 600, 1.94 rounded up = 2, so 600 divided by 2 = 300

15 (a) 0.00**8**5

(b) 0.0**9**5

(c) 0.7**5**5

16 To round to three significant figures, look at the fourth significant figure. It is 6 so round up and the answer is 0.0825.

17 To round to four significant figures, look at the fifth significant figure. It is 2 so round down and the answer is 0.6400.

18 (a) 12.855 = 12.9

(b) 1.588 = 1.59

(c) 12.587 = 12.6

Paper 2: Social context and behaviour

1 Social influence

1 (a) C Conformity

(b) B 32%

(c) A Autonomous state

2 (a) Obedience is following an order given by a person with recognised authority over you.

(b) One social factor is group size, as individuals look to others as we have a desire to be liked. Another is task difficulty which is found when we are asked to perform a task that is unfamiliar and there is no clear answer and we look to others for information.

(c) Moral strain is anxiety experienced when an individual is ordered to do something against their will.

(d) In order to reduce moral strain, the person will shift to the agentic state, relieving the moral strain as the responsibility for their actions is displaced onto the authority figure.

(e) Adorno proposed a theory and set out to measure the extent to which upbringing could affect personality factors. Children brought up by strict overbearing parents will grow up to be more obedient as they tend to be submissive to those in authority.

(f) Collective behaviour is the behaviour we display when we are in a group situation.

(g) Manchester United football fans and the London riots

3 (a) Deindividuation is the process by which individuals come to feel that they are part of a group or crowd, and so surrender their independence and autonomy.

(b) Katalina might decide not to attend the netball training session as she has an external locus of control; she is more likely to conform as she does not believe she is in control of what happens to her and may not consider the consequences of her actions. Arti has an internal locus of control and is more independent.

(c) Culture is a factor in collective behaviour as there are cultural differences in the norms and values that individuals live by. Collectivist cultures, such as China, are less affected by social loafing than individualistic cultures, such as the UK.

(d) Prosocial behaviour, such as empathy and kindness, is positive whereas antisocial behaviour, such as aggression, is negative.

4 (a) External locus of control is the belief that our behaviour is influenced by external forces such as luck or fate, whereas internal locus of control is the belief that the influence is internal and comes from the individual.

(b) To measure the effect of the type of victim on helping behaviour

(c) The sample included 4,450 men and women, 55 per cent white and 45 per cent black.

(d) A weakness is that the study wasn't very reliable as it was difficult to control all the variables; for example, the researchers could not be sure if the passengers on the train were paying attention to the situation.

(e) Presence of others and the cost of helping

2 Language, thought and communication

1 C Marking territory

2 (a) Body language is also known as kinesthetics and involves the actual movement of the body.

(b) In Piaget's theory of language and thought, at the **sensorimotor** stage the child will tend to repeat sounds and words they hear from others.

(c) The Sapir–Whorf hypothesis suggests that culture has a large impact on the way we think and the sense we make of the world. This concept is known as **linguistic determinism**.

(d) All humans categorise and remember colours the same way because we all share the same visual system. This is the **universalist** hypothesis.

(e) Eyes are perceived as more attractive when the pupils are **dilated**.

(f) Words can be combined to create an infinite number of ideas. This is known as **variety**.

(g) Verbal communication is the passing on of information using words; it can also include written communication.

(h) Personal space is the distance between ourselves and others that we feel comfortable with.

(i) The larger amount of personal space required by people with a high status is shown by their larger homes and gardens and so on. It is also suggested that our perception of personal space differs between those of similar status to us and those of a higher or lower status.

3 Caregivers need to pick up on the non-verbal cues of the baby to know what they are feeling – for example, is the baby feeling hungry, wet, too cold or too warm? This would suggest that babies have an innate set of cues that they can use at the appropriate time. Non-verbal cues may include smiling or reaching towards their caregiver.

4 Variation in recall is seen to be linked to culture and our experience of the world, and also links to schema theory. A study compared Spanish and English speakers and the difference in recall of accidental and intended events where recall is relative to the language spoken.

5 Piaget proposed a theory that language is only acquired once a child has the cognitive ability, and language reflects thinking. He suggested there were four stages in cognitive development: sensorimotor (0 to 2 years), pre-operational (2 – 7 years), concrete operational (7 – 11 years) and formal operational (11+ years) and that thought was qualitatively different at each stage which links to the sophistication of the language at each stage.

6 One function of eye contact is to regulate the flow of a conversation; the person speaking is watching the eyes of the listener for an indication that they are listening and about to interrupt, so the speaker knows when to stop talking and let the other person speak.

7 Yuki *et al.* carried out a cross-cultural study with 118 volunteer American students and 95 volunteer Japanese students. They completed a questionnaire where they were asked to rate on a scale of 1 (very sad) to 9 (very happy) the emotional expressions of six different emoticons with combinations of happy and sad eyes and mouths. The two cultures responded differently to the emoticons. The Japanese gave higher ratings to faces with happy eyes and the American participants gave higher ratings to faces with happy mouths. This shows that there are cultural differences in how emotions are expressed and interpreted in faces.

8 The research lacks ecological validity because emoticons are not the same as human faces. Another criticism is that the sample was not very representative as it only represented one age group. Older or younger age groups may interpret faces differently. The dependent variable was measured in a very simple way. Recognising emotions is a complex process and so just measuring it on a scale of 1 to 9 is not very reliable.

9 Research carried out on people who are sensory deprived supports non-verbal communication as innate, as children who are born blind and who are still able to use non-verbal cues such as smiling, shows that the non-verbal cues are innate and not learned.

10 According to Darwin's theory, behaviour that is adaptive enables survival and is passed on through the generations. Darwin's theory is based mainly on physical characteristics and evolutionary psychologists suggest that this is also the same for psychological behaviours such as non-verbal communication. Therefore, non-verbal communication may be a result of nature rather than nurture.

3 Brain and neuropsychology

1 **C** Decision making

2 (a) The **hypothalamic–pituitary–adrenal** axis is responsible for arousing the ANS in response to a threat.

(b) The **sympathetic branch** of the nervous system stimulates the adrenal gland to release adrenaline, noradrenaline and corticosteroids into the bloodstream.

(c) The increase in **adrenaline** produces the physiological reactions, such as increased heart rate and blood pressure.

(d) After the threat is gone, it takes **20 to 60 minutes** for the body to return to its pre-arousal levels.

3 (a) The **James–Lange** theory of emotion suggests that emotions are a result of physiological responses, and not their cause.

(b) The perception of **emotion-arousing** stimuli is followed by specific physiological reactions such as release of adrenaline and flight reaction.

(c) The brain interprets the specific physiological changes as the **emotion**.

(d) 'I'm **scared** because my heart is racing and I am **running away**.'

4 **B** Pre-frontal cortex

5

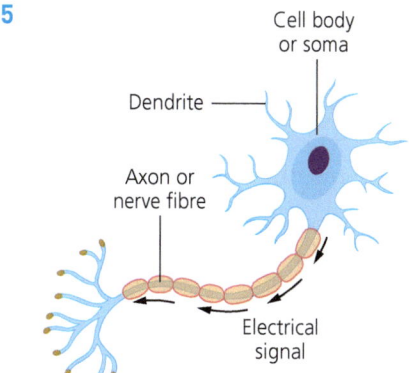

A neuron

Sensory neurons are afferent neurons, meaning they relay information to the brain only. Relay and motor neurons can carry a message in one direction only. Motor neurons carry information from the brain to the target. Relay neurons carry information from sensory neurons to motor neurons, bypassing the brain.

6 **(a) Nerve impulse** travels down an axon and reaches a synaptic terminal.

(b) This triggers the release of **neurotransmitters** and these are fired into the synaptic gap.

(c) The neurotransmitter binds with receptors on the **dendrite** of the adjacent neuron.

(d) If successfully transmitted, the neurotransmitter is taken up by the **post-synaptic** neuron. The message will continue to be passed in this way via **electrical impulses**.

7 Hebb's theory proposed that the more pre- and postsynaptic transmission occurs, the more it will strengthen the connections between the neurons involved and lead to neuronal growth. Hebb suggests that continually firing an adjacent neuron by the same neuron will eventually form a 'cell assembly' or memory trace. Hebb showed that the biological activity of the brain is related to cognitive functions supporting the area of cognitive neuroscience.

4 Psychological problems

1 **C** Lacking self-worth

2 **A** Increased aggression

3 Stigma towards mental health is lessening over time which is due to the recognition across the media of the nature of mental health problems and the number of people seeking help for their mental health. The profile of mental health issues will also lead to more open discussion in schools and in family groups and better support for the individual.

4 **(a)** Unipolar depression includes symptoms such as **low mood** and **change in sleep patterns**.

(b) The diagnosis will be made if symptoms persist for a **two-week** period.

(c) The **severity** of the illness is based on the **number** of symptoms the patient is experiencing.

(d) The more symptoms, the **higher** the severity is judged.

5 Significant mental health problems can be damaging to relationships because living with a family member who has a mental health problem can be very stressful. Mental health problems can result in difficulties coping with day-to-day life that others take for granted. This may include motivation to take part in activities that to most people bring enjoyment, such as going out for a meal with friends. Mental health problems have implications for the economy due to the cost to the NHS and other agencies which support people with mental health problems. There is a further effect on the economy because the individual may be unable to work due their mental health problems and then are not able to pay tax and national insurance contributions.

6 Serotonin is linked to sleep, appetite and mood, and patients with depression have low levels of serotonin, as they respond to anti-depressants which increase the levels of serotonin. This shows that low levels of serotonin may affect unipolar depression.

7 Cognitive behaviour therapy (CBT) recognises the importance of changing both behaviour and thinking. The role of the therapist is to help the patient identify their irrational thoughts and to change their interpretations to get rid of negative biases. The patient must change both the way they think and their behaviour. One strength of CBT is there is evidence to show it is effective; Butler *et al.* (2006) studied the results from more than 10,000 patients and found that CBT was effective in treating depression (and more successfully than anti-depressants), anxiety disorder, panic disorder and social phobia.

8 Reductionism is reducing complex phenomena to one factor, such as a biological reason; in the case of mental health improvement, that would include drug treatments as they focus on one neurotransmitter, serotonin. This can be seen as a strength as we are able to measure precisely the levels of serotonin and are able to control the dosage of the selective serotonin reuptake inhibitors. However, it could be argued that drug treatments alone are not effective and the reductionist viewpoint is too narrow.

Exam practice answers

Paper 1: Cognition and behaviour

1 Memory

1 (a) One factor that may affect the accuracy of memory is context. [1 mark]

(b) Context affects the accuracy of memory because when we store a new memory, we also store information about the situation. When we come to the same situation again, these context retrieval cues can trigger the memory. Retrieval cues can be:
- External, such as cues in the environment, e.g. smell, place etc.
- Internal, such as our physical or emotional state.

Recall of information will be more accurate if it occurs in the same context that learning took place. [3 marks]

2 Most research into memory involves participants learning lists of words under laboratory conditions. This is not what people usually have to do in everyday life. Therefore, the results lack ecological validity.

Research into false memory often involves deception, as participants are not aware that their memory is being manipulated and this raises ethical concerns.

Research into memory is usually conducted as laboratory experiments using small samples of student participants, thus the results are unrepresentative of the memories of the wider population. [4 marks]

3 Marks for this question: AO2 = 4 and AO3 = 2 [6 marks]

AO2 marks: (2 + 2) marks for identification of a suitable experimental design that is justified and for a description of a memory task and the data to be collected. AO3 marks: up to two marks for a description of the expected results.

Method and design: the research would be a laboratory experiment having a repeated measures design. A repeated measures design would be used so that there are no participant variables which would affect recall of the words. [2 marks]

Task: 20 participants would be shown 12 numbers one at a time and asked to repeat them. Each number would be one digit longer than the previous number, 3, 45, 367, 6769, 7643, 93427, etc.

Data: a record would be kept of the position in the list of the **last number** that was correctly recalled. For example, if the participant did not correctly recall the 7-digit number, they would be allocated a score of 6. When all 20 participants have been tested, an average score would be calculated. [2 marks]

Expected result: since previous research shows the capacity of STM to be seven plus or minus two digits, it is expected that the average score would be between five and nine. [2 marks]

4 [3 marks]

Table 1.2 Three descriptions of processes linked to memory

Holding information in the memory system	C
Changing information so that it can be stored in memory	A
Recovering information from memory	B

5 Sundip is basing her revision on the multi-store model of memory. In the multi-store model, information is rehearsed in STM and, if rehearsed enough, is transferred to LTM. In this model of memory, sensory information is perceived and is then transferred to STM, **where it is maintained by rehearsal** before being transferred to LTM. [2 marks]

6 The aspect of memory as an active process is **forgetting due to retrieval failure**. [1 mark]

7 Marks for this question: AO1 = 4 and AO3 = 5 [9 marks]

Suggested answer:

AO1: Loftus and Pickrell: Lost in the Mall

Aim: The aim of the study was to see if suggestion could create false memories.

Method: There were 24 participants (3 males and 21 females) ranging in age from 18 to 53. For each participant, a relative was also contacted. The participants were given four short stories about childhood events that had been obtained from their relatives. Three of the stories were true and one was false. The false story was about getting lost in a shopping mall and being rescued by an elderly woman. The false story included information such as who usually went on shopping trips with the child so that the false story sounded realistic.

Each participant was asked to read each story and then write down what they remembered about each event. A week later each participant was interviewed about the stories and were told that one of the stories was false and asked to guess which one.

Results: Participants remembered 68 per cent of the 72 true events. Six of the participants (25 per cent) recalled the false story. 19 out of the 24 participants correctly identified the lost in the mall memory as false. [4 marks]

Conclusion: Just being told about an event can create a false memory.

AO3: Evaluation can include critical appraisals that are positive and/or negative. For example:

One weakness of the study is that the false memory event is not very traumatic and it may be easier to create a false memory for a harmless event than for an untrue trauma. Another weakness is deception when participants are told untrue stories and ethical issues arise when participants are left with an implanted false memory. A strength is that the research is useful as it can be applied to improve the way witnesses to crimes are interviewed so that questions are not asked in such a way that will implant a false memory. [5 marks]

2 Perception

1 D Sensation [1 mark]

2 A Ambiguity [1 mark]

3 B Occlusion [1 mark]

4 The monocular depth cue is linear perspective. Linear perspective is used by artists as a depth cue in which, because parallel lines in the real world never meet, lines such as the edges of the road are drawn appearing to get narrower (to converge) in the distance, giving the appearance of the road going into the distance. [2 marks]

5 One binocular depth cue is retinal disparity. Each eye views a slightly different angle of an object. If an object is far away, the disparity of that image falling on both retinas will be small. If the object is close, the disparity will be large. [3 marks]

6 Gregory argued that perception is a constructive process which relies on top-down processing as the brain has to guess what a person sees based on past experiences (nurture not nature). According to Gregory, sensory information is combined with our memories about the world which we have learned as a result of experience, so that our perceptions of the world are hypotheses based on past experiences. [4 marks]

7 Marks for this question: AO3 = 5.

Evidence from research shows that factors such as expectation can affect perception, supporting Gregory's theory that perception is actively constructed.

Also, visual illusions show that people apply their stored knowledge of the world to interpreting 2D representations which shows that perception is influenced by prior knowledge.

However, Gibson's bottom-up theory challenges the constructivist theory, arguing that perception is innate and that the information received by the retina is detailed enough to be able to interpret the sensation without inference. Also, most people perceive the world in a similar way which suggests that most information is not constructed by our minds.

Finally, if perception is about experience then we should not see the same visual illusion the second time because we should have learned that what we 'see' is not 'there' but this rarely happens. [5 marks]

3 Development

1 A The child thinks in an abstract way. [1 mark]

2 B 2–7 [1 mark]

3 Piaget suggested that teachers should take an age-related approach by presenting opportunities for learning matched to the stage of cognitive development [1 mark], for example by providing sand and water and modelling clay for children in the pre-operational stage to support the development of the ability to conserve [1 mark], or by providing objects to manipulate during the concrete operational stage to support the development of mental reasoning.

4 Possible answers:

Piaget's theory has been criticised because it is based on small and unrepresentative samples/his own children and he did not standardise his methods.

Piaget's theory has been criticised because the tasks he set were confusing to children. For example, in standard conservation tasks, he asked children the same questions many times which might have led children to change their answers and get the answers wrong.

Piaget's theory has been criticised because he set fixed 'age-related' stages for development of cognitive skills that underestimate the age at which children acquire object permanence and/or the ability to conserve. [4 marks]

5 **(a)** Fixed mindset [1 mark]

(b) Marks for this question: AO1 = 3 and AO2 = 3 [6 marks]

AO1: Mindset theory is a theory of motivation and explains how students can achieve success in their learning. Students are described as having generally one of two types of mindset. Fixed mindset students believe their ability is fixed, comes from talent, and is probably genetic. This means that when faced with a challenge, the student with this mindset often 'gives up'.

Growth mindset students believe ability is due to learning and that learning takes time and effort, being prepared to ask for help and to practise. This means that when faced with a challenge in their learning, the student with this mindset will keep trying which increases the likelihood of success. [3 marks]

AO2: Michelle seems to have a fixed mindset about her ability in maths, stating that 'I am not very clever at maths and never will be' which suggests her inability to do maths is fixed and that no amount of effort or revision on her part will change that. [3 marks]

6 Marks for this question: AO1 = 3, AO2 = 3, AO3 = 3
[9 marks]

Suggested answer:

AO1: Mindset theory is a theory of motivation and explains how students can achieve success in their learning. Students are described as having generally one of two types of mindset. Fixed mindset students believe their ability is fixed, comes from talent, and is probably genetic. This means that when faced with a challenge, the student with this mindset often 'gives up'.

Growth mindset students believe ability is due to learning and that learning takes time and effort, being prepared to ask for help and to practise. This means that when faced with a challenge in their learning, the student with this mindset will keep trying which increases the likelihood of success. [3 marks]

AO2: Phyliss seems to have a fixed mindset about her ability to learn French, telling Benito, 'You'll get an A because you were born good at learning languages, but I wasn't, so there's no point me trying', so it's clear she thinks that the ability to learn French is 'not in her nature'. Benito has a growth mindset about his ability to learn French as he says, 'I wasn't any good at first, but I've practised and practised my French and that's why I'm better now, but it's been hard work', recognising that his ability in French is the result of all the effort he has put into learning. [3 marks]

AO3: There is evidence to support Dweck's Mindset Theory. Dweck showed how the type of praise given by teachers can affect the mindset of students. Person-oriented praise, for example 'you are good at this' leads students to attribute their success, and more importantly failure, to something beyond their control, whereas process-oriented praise, for example 'that was a good way to answer that question' teaches students to believe their success or failure was

due to amount of effort. Hattie and Marzano found that students who believed they would master fractions were more likely to do so, while students who believed they were poor readers were less likely to improve their reading. All in all, Mindset Theory is useful as it shows that if students can change their belief system, they can be motivated to improve their academic outcomes. [3 marks]

7 (a) A learning style is the preferred way in which an individual approaches a learning situation. [1 mark]

(b) Marks for this question: AO1 = 3 and AO3 = 3
[6 marks]

AO1: Having a verbaliser or a visualiser learning style describes the degree to which individuals tend to represent information as words (verbaliser) or as images (visualiser). Some research suggests that if students are verbalisers, they learn best from text-based material while students who are visualisers learn best from pictorially-presented material. This suggests that if there is a mismatch between a student's preferred learning style and the way information to be learned is presented, learning will be adversely affected. [3 marks]

AO3: Learning styles are measured using questionnaires which may not be valid. Also, whether a student prefers information presented visually or verbally may depend on what is being learned. Willingham criticised the theory of learning styles as being unscientific. He suggests that whether or not a student understands a lesson depends not on the learning style of the child but on the knowledge the child brings to the lesson or other factors. Willingham suggests that rather than considering 'learning styles', teachers should use the lesson content's best modality so that if students are to learn what something looks like, then the presentation should be visual. [3 marks]

4 Research methods

1 (a) A laboratory experiment [1 mark]

(b) The IV is the difference in the way the numbers were presented – with gaps as in PF5 83 YZ or without gaps as in PF583YZ. [1 mark]

(c) The DV is the number of correctly recalled letters and numbers in the right position in each number plate. [1 mark]

(d) The way the number plates are presented will have no effect on the number of correctly recalled letters and numbers in the right position in each number plate.

OR: There will be no difference in the number of correctly recalled letters and numbers in the right position in each number plate between those who are shown the number plates with no gaps and those who are shown the number plates with gaps. [2 marks]

(e) Condition A total is 250 so the mean is 250 divided by 10 = 25 [1 mark]

To calculate the mean: $30 + 25 + 22 + 20 + 33 + 25 + 28 + 29 + 15 + 23 = \frac{250}{10} = 25$

Condition B total is 170 so the mean is 170 divided by 10 = 17 [1 mark]

(f) Condition B range is 23 (highest score) minus 12 (lowest score) = 11 [2 marks]

(g) Marks for this question: AO2 = 1 and AO3 = 2 [3 marks]

AO2: The mean is higher for Condition A (25 as opposed to 17). [1 mark]

AO3: The higher mean suggests that people recall the number plates written in small groups (chunks) more accurately than when they are presented as one string of numbers. This might suggest chunked information improves accuracy of recall. [2 marks]

(h) Marks for this question: AO2 = 2

The range in Condition B is smaller than the range in Condition A (17 compared to 25) which might suggest that there is more consistency (similarity) in the recall of the number plates in Condition B. [2 marks]

(i) Marks for this question: AO2 = 3

Clear description containing all of the following points (3 marks); reasonable description but lacking in detail (2 marks); very brief description, for example: put all the names in a hat and pick out 20 (1 mark).

Obtain a list of all 200 names of the psychology students. Write each name on a slip of paper and fold the slip. Put all the folded slips into a box. Ask someone to pull out 20 of the slips. The 20 psychology students selected will become the random sample.

2 (a) Marks for this question: AO2 = 4

Informative title (1 mark); correct labelling of both axes (1 mark); correct scaling of both axes (1 mark); correct plotting of the results (1 mark).

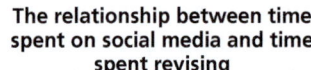

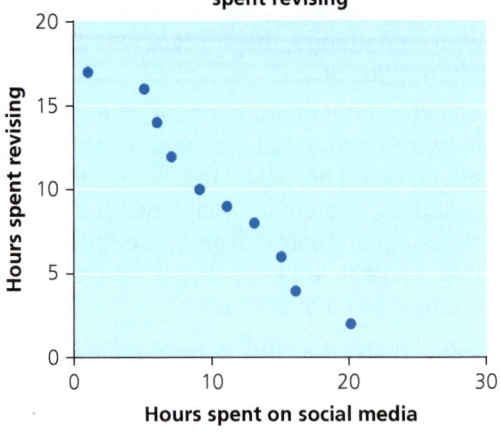

The relationship between time spent on social media and time spent revising

(b) A Negative correlation [1 mark]

(c) Marks for this question: AO3 = 3

Appropriate reference to the results and direction of the relationship effectiveness (1 mark); appropriate explanation (2 marks).

Suggested answer:

The results suggest that there is a negative relationship between the amount of time students spend on social media [1 mark] and time spent revising and that students who spend more time on social media will spend less time revising. [2 marks]

Paper 2: Social context and behaviour

1 Social influence

1 (a) Task difficulty [1 mark]

(b) One reason for conformity is when an individual is asked to perform a task that is unfamiliar and there is no clear answer. If the task is difficult and the individual is unsure of the correct answer, they will look to others for information as they have a desire to be right. When Asch made the comparison lines more similar in his variation, the rate of conformity increased. [3 marks]

2 One criticism of research into conformity is that studies lack ecological validity, for example in Asch's study participants were in a laboratory and they had an artificial line judgement task. This would not reflect how we experience conformity in everyday life. Also, the sample in most studies are male and therefore results cannot be generalised to females. [4 marks]

3 Camelia is on her way to work and is wearing a new coat. Helping may mean that she is late for

work and will be in trouble and she might damage her new coat which would be a cost, and that would outweigh the gain of feeling good about helping. [3 marks]

4 Nancy would see the teacher as a legitimate authority and will obey as the teacher is present. In Milgram's study the participants obeyed the experimenter as they saw them as a legitimate authority. [2 marks]

5 Deindividuation [1 mark]

6 Marks for this question: AO1 = 3 and AO3 = 3
[6 marks]

AO1: Piliavin carried out an observational study on the New York subway train. A victim staggered forward and collapsed; in one condition he carried a cane and in the second condition he smelled of alcohol and carried a bag. Helping behaviour was measured by the number of times spontaneous help was offered, how long it took before help was offered and the race of the victim which gained most help. [3 marks]

AO3: A strength of the study is that it is high in ecological validity as it took place on the subway in New York, which is a real-life environment. Therefore, we can apply the findings beyond the setting of the study. A weakness is that the study wasn't very reliable as it was difficult to control all the variables; for example, the researchers could not be sure if the passengers on the train were paying attention to the situation. [3 marks]

7 Adorno proposed a theory and set out to measure the extent to which upbringing could affect personality factors. Authoritarian personality was proposed by Adorno where children brought up by strict overbearing parents will grow up to be more submissive to those in authority.
[2 marks]

8 People with an authoritarian personality will grow up to be more obedient as they tend to be submissive to those in authority. Milgram compared F scores (a measure for authoritarian personality) between obedient and disobedient participants and found higher levels in obedient participants. [3 marks]

2 Language, thought and communication

1 The table shows there is a difference between Argentinian and British participants where the average difference in personal space is lower for the Argentinians at 76cm. Research has shown there are cultural differences in how we perceive personal space, for example Argentinians have the lowest personal space. The results would support this difference. [3 marks]

2 C Postural echo [1 mark]

3 Marks for this question: AO3 = 3

A strength of the study is that it inspired other research to be carried out in animal communication and the original study has been replicated increasing the validity. However, later research with bees suggests that rather than communication, the bees have a cognitive ability for navigation. [3 marks]

4 One difference between an open and closed posture in non-verbal communication is how the arms are positioned; in closed posture, they would be folded and in open posture, down by your side. [3 marks]

5 Piaget proposed a theory that language is only acquired once a child has the cognitive ability and language reflects thinking; and as thinking is different at each stage, language will be different.
[4 marks]

6 Marks for this question: AO3 = 5

The Sapir–Whorf hypothesis is supported by evidence from different cultures that show how words they used were specific to their location. For example, the Hopi Indians in the US have one word to incorporate 'insect' and 'plane' as they have no need to show the difference between them. However, there were flaws in Whorf's research as he did not actually research directly with the Hopi Indians and his research is seen as anecdotal rather than experimental. [5 marks]

7 Marking and defending territory – for example, cats and dogs scent-mark boundaries of territory, and male dogs urinate on trees to communicate and mark their territory. Warning about danger – blackbirds call loudly, rapidly and repeatedly to communicate danger, rabbits thump their paws to warn other rabbits of possible predators.
[4 marks]

8 One function of eye contact is to regulate the flow of a conversation; the person speaking is watching the eyes of the listener for an indication that they are listening and about to interrupt, so the speaker knows when to stop talking and let the other person speak. [3 marks]

9 Marks for this question: AO1 = 3 and AO3 = 3

AO1: Social learning theory starts with the idea that we observe and copy behaviours of the same species. Social learning theory argues that non-verbal communication is a learned behaviour rather than a natural instinctive one. Humans observe others; they pay attention consciously and unconsciously to the behaviour of role models around them. They then imitate those around them who they admire or love.

AO3: However, social learning theory cannot really explain why children brought up in the same environment can have quite different ways of communicating. For example, two brothers raised by the same parents in the same community can have very different ways of expressing themselves. [6 marks]

3 Brain and neuropsychology

1 B The occipital lobe [1 mark]

2 One strength is that Penfield could access live participants to show the direct effects of stimulating different parts of the brain. This increased the ecological validity of the study. However, the study used the case study method and all of the patients were epileptic, so the findings can't be generalised to people who do not have epilepsy. [4 marks]

3 Sensory neurons are afferent neurons, meaning they relay information to the brain only. They respond to information through the senses, for example touching something hot and activating motor neurons to respond by pulling the hand away. [2 marks]

4 (a) Marks for this question: AO2 = 4

When the vampire jumps out, it creates fear in Jenna and Christian. Their response is the fight or flight response. In a fight or flight situation, the sympathetic nervous system prepares the body and so both Jenna and Christian's heart rate quickens to get more blood to the muscles, blood flow is diverted from the organs so that digestion is reduced and pupils dilate for better vision. Christian jumps out of his seat to show he is prepared to run. [4 marks]

(b) The theory suggests that emotions are a result of these physiological responses, and not their cause. The perception of emotion-arousing stimuli is followed by specific physiological reactions such as release of adrenaline and flight reaction. The brain interprets the specific physiological changes as the emotion, 'I'm scared because my heart is racing, and I am running away.' [4 marks]

(c) Marks for this question: AO1 = 1 and AO3 = 3

AO1: One criticism of the James–Lange's theory of emotion is that it ignores cognitive effects on emotions. [1 mark]

AO3: Maranon (1924) found that physiological arousal is not enough to cause emotion. Only around two-thirds of participants who were injected with adrenaline reported physical symptoms. Schachter and Singer (1962) suggest that emotions are the result of not just physiological changes, but there is also a cognitive component as we interpret the situation as well. [3 marks]

5 (a) The nerve impulse travels down an axon and reaches the synaptic terminal. This triggers the release of a neurotransmitter(s) which is fired into the synaptic gap. The neurotransmitter(s) binds with receptors on the dendrite of the adjacent neuron and if successfully transmitted the neurotransmitter(s) is taken up by the post-synaptic neuron. The message will continue to be passed in this way via electrical impulses. [4 marks]

(b) **Excitatory neurotransmitters** conduct the action potential (AP) to release a neurotransmitter and they affect the postsynaptic neurons. All excitatory neurotransmitters cause sodium ions to flow in and the cell becomes less negative on the inside. **Inhibitory neurotransmitters**: if an AP goes down the synaptic knob of another neuron and releases an inhibitory neurotransmitter, it is going to be activating different receptor sites on the cell membrane of the postsynaptic cell. [5 marks]

4 Psychological problems

1 D Hallucinations [1 mark]

2 C Active avoidance of the substance to reduce the behaviour [1 mark]

3 Marks for this question: AO1 = 4 and AO3 = 4

AO1: Wiles carried out a study to test the effectiveness of CBT in patients with drug treatment resistant depression. Participants were allocated to two groups; 234 received CBT alongside their normal treatment (drug and medical routines), 235 received their normal treatment. CBT was carried out by a trained therapist and the participants had 12 one-hour sessions. The results show that over the course of 46 months, 43 per cent of those who had received CBT had improved, reporting at least a 50 per cent reduction in symptoms of depression, compared with 27 per cent who continued with their usual care alone. CBT is an effective treatment that can be used alongside drug treatments for patients with depression. [4 marks]

AO3: One strength is that the study is longitudinal, and researchers were able to follow patients over a 12-month period. This allowed the researchers to follow the same participants throughout and to assess the participants at different stages of the treatment. However, not all the participants attended all the sessions. This weakens the argument that CBT is an effective treatment. [4 marks]

4 Marks for this question: AO1 = 3 and AO3 = 3

AO1: Biological explanations for depression argue that the cause is linked to nature and genetically determined. From this perspective depression is purely biological and part of our DNA which determines our physiology and neural activity. Depression is linked to an imbalance in the neurotransmitter serotonin which is linked to sleep, appetite and mood. Patients with depression have low levels of serotonin, as they respond to anti-depressants which increase the levels of serotonin. [3 marks]

AO3: In post-mortem studies, McNeal and Cimbolic (1986) found lower levels of serotonin by-products in the cerebrospinal fluid of previously suicidal patients, suggesting lower levels of serotonin in the brain. This shows that there is a link between serotonin and depression. However, this ignores the effects of the environment where children acquire negative schemas which are activated to generate cognitive biases. This means that both nature and nurture could play a role in unipolar depression. [3 marks]

5 The most common antidepressants used for depression are selective serotonin reuptake inhibitors (SSRIs) such as fluoxetine that block the reuptake of serotonin from the synaptic gap, causing levels of the neurotransmitter to increase. These relieve the symptoms of low mood, sleep disturbance and low energy levels and treat unipolar depression. [4 marks]

6 **Addiction** is a repetitive habit pattern that increases the risk of disease and/or associated personal and social problems. Addictive behaviours are often experienced subjectively as a 'loss of control' – the behaviour continues to occur despite volitional attempts to abstain or moderate use. **Dependence** can be physical in nature and is usually experienced with addiction to substances, such as nicotine. Attempts to give up will lead to physical symptoms such as tolerance and withdrawal. [5 marks]

7 Marks for this question: AO1 = 2 and AO3 = 4

AO1: The genetic model suggests that there is a genetic disposition towards addictive behaviour and that an addictive personality may be genetically determined. Research in this area analyses the genetic structure of the individual and their role in the prevalence of addictive behaviours. [2 marks]

AO3: Hughes (1986) compared two groups of adolescents. One group lived with family members who smoked, and the other group lived with family members who did not smoke. Findings showed that 52 per cent of those who lived with smokers smoked compared to 20 per cent of those living with non-smokers. This is further supported by adoption studies. Hall *et al.* (2002) found a strong association between adoptees and their biological siblings smoking. This supports the idea that addiction is genetically linked and due to nature.

However, peer pressure has been linked to first time use of nicotine and recreational drugs, but peer pressure is more prevalent in teenage years and decreases with age. McAlister (1984) found that increased levels of smoking were linked to peer pressure and encouragement which is rewarding. This suggests that environmental factors may also influence addiction as well as nature. [4 marks]

8 Self-management programmes work on the basis that social support can help with addictions, particularly as all the members of the group are going through the same process or may be further along the process and able to provide motivation. Alcoholics Anonymous and Narcotics Anonymous use the 12-step recovery programme. The steps progress from 'we admit we have no control over the alcohol and that our lives have become unmanageable', to 'we have had a spiritual awakening as the result of these steps'. [4 marks]